FUTURE TENSE

ZIMMER GUNSUL FRASCA

Foreword By **Robert Frasca**

Essay By **Joseph Giovannini**

Balcony Press | Los Angeles

Contents

Foreword

Robert Frasca, FAIA

IN THE EIGHT YEARS SINCE the last collection of our work was published, there has been a seismic shift (as compared to a glacial one) in the projects we have completed. While any collection of buildings by the same group of individuals will invariably adapt to changing conditions, our work's evolution has been quite substantial. This was brought about less by stylistic predilections on our part and more by the broad variety of our clients, their programmatic needs, and the places in which we have built.

IT IS ALWAYS GRATIFYING to see the completion of projects that have had long gestation periods. We were involved with the Mark O. Hatfield Clinical Research Center at the National Institutes of Health, for example, for more than 10 years, from our winning competition entry to the dedication. The design fulfilled the original intentions, the proof being the testimonials we continue to receive from those who use the Bethesda, Maryland, facility. On the other hand, the 1.1 million-square-foot Conference Center for The Church of Jesus Christ of Latter-day Saints in Salt Lake City was completed in three and a half years, from initial design studies to occupancy. When we watched 21,000 people occupy the great hall and others stroll the six-acre roof garden at the initial conference, it was a marvel for us to behold.

ANOTHER PROJECT, the Portland International Airport, has had a 40-year evolution. Because we have had the luxury of working there for that extensive period of time (beginning with the first building addition after the original terminal was built), we have been able to provide an element of design continuity and clarity that is lacking in other airports that have gone through similar evolutions. Our almost 20-year tenure at Seattle's Fred Hutchinson Cancer Research Center has produced the same result. From the initial campus master plan to the most recent addition (the Robert M. Arnold Public Health Sciences Building), each building becomes another cohesive element in completing the initial vision for that campus. The same can be said for the Washington State University campus in Vancouver: Our master plan celebrated the beauty and uniqueness of the site, and each building makes the whole greater than the sum of its parts.

WE CONTINUE TO DESIGN the broadest range of building types, and that diversity continues to raise the level of everything we do. In the most profound ways, one building type informs another, and that is best explained by the obvious fact that they are all used by people. Granted, these people are involved in very different activities—conducting research in a laboratory, practicing law in a civic building, or recovering in a hospital—but fundamentally they have similar basic reactions to their surroundings.

THAT SAID, even the most casual observer of our work will note clear differences within the same building type. In all cases, the work is a direct response to the site, the culture, and environment, among other factors. Take, for example, the Chemical Sciences Building at the University of Arizona and the Fitzpatrick Center at Duke University: Although they have similar programs, the facilities' dissimilitude reflects the fact that they are in very different places, with very different climates.

OFTEN, WHEN WE DESIGN a building that is especially unique for its purpose, it begets other buildings that have the same purpose. An example is Portland's Doernbecher Children's Hospital, completed almost

10 years ago. Its success allowed us to design children's hospitals in Denver, Los Angeles, Chicago, and Dallas. Similar among these facilities are the functional and qualitative aspects common to all children's hospitals. However, since the locations and program sizes vary, we refined those qualities, celebrating what is unique at each. The same can be said for the Science Center of Iowa, an offspring of the Oregon Museum of Science and Industry and the California Science Center. Each building has its own character, never to be duplicated—at least by us.

RESEARCH BUILDINGS THAT ARE directed toward the study and cure of human disease continue to be an important part of what we do. The Mortimer B. Zuckerman Research Center at Memorial Sloan-Kettering Cancer Center in New York is the most recent and prominent example. However, the Leichtag Family Foundation Biomedical Research Building at UC San Diego, the Thomas W. Keating Bioresearch and Medical Research Building at the University of Arizona, the transdisciplinary Natural Science and Engineering Building for the University of Texas at Dallas, and the Biomedical Research Building at Oregon Health & Science University are equally innovative in many ways. Examining them on even a superficial level clearly shows that each was created to suit how the science is conducted at that particular place.

EXTENSIONS OF THE MEDICAL research work we do are buildings for translational research, in which the patient is in proximity to the laboratory. This is the premise of the clinical center at NIH, and replicated on a smaller scale with a slight twist at the Rebecca and John Moores UCSD Cancer Center in San Diego. In this case, the research, outpatient clinics, and population studies are co-located around a "mesa" so that their work together can be highly interactive, with a greater potential for extraordinary results.

THE MERGING OF THE SCIENCES is a phenomenon that can be witnessed in some of our most recent work. The Stanley Hall replacement project at UC Berkeley is a bioengineering building that brings together the physical and biological sciences with the computer sciences and engineering to unravel puzzles heretofore unapproachable in medical science. The Fitzpatrick Center at Duke University is similar in its multidisciplinary nature but unites a different set of components. Cornell's Duffield Hall, which focuses on nanotechnology, is "glued onto" the electrical engineering facility, resulting in a multilevel interactive center for all the disciplines that surround the redesigned quadrangle. Another example is the science complex at Williams College, which brings together in an almost seamless fashion 19th- and 20th-century buildings around a central library and connects to new laboratories.

THE LARGER, MORE COMPLEX research centers on which we work are often informed by the smaller ones. The biomedical engineering building at the University of Michigan, a 30,000-square-foot addition that doubled the size of a pre-existing building, has a configuration of zoned laboratory and support spaces that results in open labs with enclosed noise- and heat-generating areas. The 85,000-square-foot laboratory for the Carnegie Institution in Baltimore is tailored to a unique research culture that promotes a highly collaborative approach.

INFRASTRUCTURE CONTINUES TO BE an important component of what we do. Many projects of this type are in process, but the recently completed San Diego State University Transit Center is one example of how urban places and campus communities are being transformed by transit. Relatively new to our portfolio are multifamily housing projects. The Eliot residential tower in Portland, the first of several similar programs to be completed, describes how a direct expression of the program of the interior units, when artfully expressed on the exterior, can display an energy that cannot be achieved in any other way.

THERE IS OTHER RECENT WORK that represents a broader range of programs, such as the Gerdin Business Building at Iowa State University, the Exposition Park Intergenerational Community Center in Los Angeles, and the Federal Courthouse in Santa Ana. It is this diversity that fuels everything we do.

NUMEROUS PROJECTS FOR the U.S. State Department have taken us outside the United States. One such project is represented in this book: the U.S. Consulate Compound in the outskirts of Istanbul. Its exterior appearance is formidable, in compliance with State Department security criteria; however, the design is indicative of its location, with interior spaces organized around a sunlit courtyard, a classic regional configuration. The resulting building provides a sense of tranquility for its occupants.

IN ALL OF OUR PROJECTS there is a commitment to build beautiful rooms. That motive is central to every building we design, whether it is integral to the architecture or carried out in the detail of the furnishings. Our interiors practice is represented here in discrete projects for two law firms and our own offices in Los Angeles.

SUSTAINABILITY HAS BEEN an important design generator for us. This began in the 1970s with the first energy crisis; when conservation ceased to be a national priority, we continued with that agenda. Now there is no question that sustainability should be central to what we do as a society, and we have taken an active role. Many of the projects that demonstrate that commitment are currently in design or construction, such as the J. Craig Venter Institute in La Jolla, California. Completed projects such as the LEED Platinum-certified environmental science building at UC Santa Barbara, the Gold-certified U.S. Environmental Protection Agency Region 8 Headquarters in Denver and engineering building at Portland State University, and the Silver-certified Fitzpatrick Center at Duke are examples of how energy conservation can be achieved seamlessly in a variety of circumstances.

WE ARE ENTERING our fifth decade under the present incarnation of our firm. The transition of leadership has been smooth, and the future has never been more promising. The contributions from everyone in all offices are evident in our work. New offices appear where the opportunities take us. We continue to work at our profession as both an art and a science, inseparable in thought and execution. We hope that all who look at this collection will understand and appreciate what it was we set out to do and the qualities evident in the final results.

Future Tense

Joseph Giovannini

ZIMMER GUNSUL FRASCA HAS A LONG HISTORY of designing iconic structures, but beyond producing a defining visual image, the architects design buildings that will shape the culture of their clients. As Churchill famously said, "We shape our buildings, and afterwards our buildings shape us." Doss Mabe, one of the design partners of ZGF, makes a corollary statement when he asks his clients, "Where do you want to be in ten years?" That is, what kind of building can we, as architects, design that will help your organization become what it wants and needs to be?

SOME ARCHITECTS IMPORT A WELL-KNOWN, well-practiced language to a commission, but ZGF prefers conversation to language: The architects cultivate a dialogue with clients, and in the to-and-fro of ideas and ideals, facts and goals, a design gradually emerges. Architecture for the firm—which has offices in Portland, Oregon; Seattle; Los Angeles; Washington, DC; and New York—is not a pre-established assumption, and certainly not an "ism," but a process: The architects start a discussion that will yield a building that neither they nor clients could have predicted before shaking hands. The architects eschew the notion of signature and brand in favor of sensitivity and receptivity. Design for them has become an interactive process; rather than staking a position vis-à-vis a project, they engage clients in a relationship. Not, "Here's what I can bring you," but "What are you looking for in a building?" How can the architects harness their creative abilities to the motors of the project? How can they cultivate, in Doss Mabe's words, "its soul"?

ZGF BASES ITS PRACTICE IN RESEARCH, and the research starts with what the firm calls "culture charrettes," during which the architects enter into a "deep interviewing" process, sometimes involving hundreds of the client's staff members. Most of these clients are institutional or corporate—groups with an identifiable character—and the architects immerse themselves in the clients' culture to help them become the institution or corporation they want to be. "The work would be less interesting if we didn't engage them, because that's where the ideas come from," says Mabe.

THE ETHIC AND ETHOS OF RESEARCH reaches beyond the clients to the culture of the ZGF office itself. The firm has organized an internal initiative focused on applied research. If the designers need, for example, a wall on a building facing west that must resist heavy solar heat gain while permitting a view, or if they are trying to "green" a roof, they work with researchers in the office who act, effectively, as environmental consultants.

THE COMBINATION OF ACADEMIA and the construction industry offers a dumbfounding amount of information, from raw product specs to breaking news. Moreover, changing codes and increasing public and professional awareness have planted environmental issues at the foreground of the profession, with a concomitant influx of new products. In-house researchers capture, process, and digest the incoming information so that the architects can factor it integrally into a design, working it pro-actively rather than passively into the concept and fabric of the buildings, explains technical design partner Jan Willemse. "Whether it's patinated stainless steel, corrugated glass, or any other new kind of glass, we need a way to understand, absorb, and formalize the information," Willemse adds. "We research collectively." Whether based in in-house research or the culture charrettes, the emphasis on research predisposes the firm toward the future, and acknowledges the inevitability of change.

Agents of Change

ZGF BUILDINGS ARE CRISP AND TAUT, layered and formally complex, and consistently handsome. But looks belie their architectural IQ, which is embedded, out of sight, in the floor plan, materials, systems, internal urbanism, and patterns of socialization. Without giving up its pursuit of the kind of design excellence that can produce iconic "destination" buildings, the firm has shifted, in incremental steps, toward an information-based cultural practice. The shift has occurred during a learning curve arcing through several highly instructive projects with clients who were driven by the necessity and desire for change.

IN 1959, NORM ZIMMER STARTED what was then a small firm in Portland, attracting other founding partners Robert Frasca in design and Brooks Gunsul in technology. They collectively expanded the firm into the Northwest and California, and then nationally. ZGF now operates as a network, able to shift resources and services as needed between offices. The firm is simultaneously local, national, and international.

IN SEVERAL VERY ACTIVE DECADES, ZGF expanded to 15 partners and produced many award-winning projects. But a turning point for ZGF, relative to its role as an agent for cultural change among its clients, came more than a decade ago, when the Food and Drug Administration approached the firm with a commission, and a problem.

THE FDA'S SOUTHERN CALIFORNIA REGIONAL OFFICE, housed in separate locations, had two corresponding divisions: investigators, who brought in food samples from the field, and lab people, who tested the samples at the bench. The FDA initiated a policy of hiring biologists who performed both roles, and decided to build a headquarters that would merge both divisions within a single, undivided building. Here, discussions with the clients—who were essentially trying to create a culture of cooperation between divisions that had previously had little interaction—would deeply affect the design in a way that could shape the institution. Letting the clients speak from the couch in a self-analytical process led to new formal arrangements that catalyzed the integration.

ZGF HAD BUILT MANY LABORATORY FACILITIES. But this commission represented one of the firm's initial opportunities in a series of research buildings that would break down the barrier between offices and labs, opening up the relationship between them. At the FDA, instead of erecting an opaque barrier between the divisions, the architects brought them together via a glass wall whose transparency allowed colleagues to see one another working on the other side of what had been a great divide.

BEYOND PUTTING OFFICES AND BENCHES in close proximity with high visibility, the architects factored social interaction into the floor plan and organization, with common stairwells and circulation that pooled staff. As a result of integrating the units within the FDA, the architects cultivated an interior urbanism within the larger outside context of an automobile culture that supports very little pedestrian life. The initial interviewing process yielded a building that the architects had engineered for an enriched interior life.

THIS INTERACTIVITY BETWEEN CLIENT AND ARCHITECT marked a change from the typical top-down relationship, in which architects act as authority figures. In the kind of collaborative process ZGF has been known for, the architects offered expertise but did not pretend to have absolute knowledge: Ideas would simply surface in the flow of discussion, and the soul of the building emerged as a registration of an institutional character.

HAVING WORKED ON THE MULTI-PHASE RENOVATION of the Portland International Airport from 1970 to 2002, ZGF was engaged by the Port of Portland to design its new headquarters at the airport. The architects again focused on understanding the culture rather than just the bottom-line statistics of the functional program. As with the FDA, the Port comprised two entities—the aviation and port divisions—and a new general manager initiated a program to break down the boundaries between the fiefs. Melding the aviation and the port divisions in the One Port program meant that more efficient teams could work on specific projects. Once again, scores of staff members were involved in ZGF's culture charrettes. "Building a new building is an opportunity to think about who you are, how you work, what you want to become," says managing partner Bob Packard. "You can throw off current constraints and try new things, and create a physical environment that catalyzes and supports change." In other words, architecture could be implemented as a tool to restructure program.

WHAT EMERGED FROM THE INTERVIEWS was the Port staff and administration's desire to create a very open environment with blurred boundaries that offered some degree of privacy and a great deal of flexibility, as the staff needed to work at various times in small and large groups. The concept demanded a dynamic environment that could anticipate an unpredictable future in which change itself is the main constant.

UNTIL RECENTLY, THE TREND was to design buildings with short life expectancies, disposable once the mortgage is amortized. The new Port of Portland headquarters was positing another paradigm, one of permanent institutional change in a building designed to accommodate, facilitate, and even induce change long beyond amortization. The fast-evolving global economy was forcing institutions like the Port of Portland into perpetual re-invention, and buildings conceived as a stage on which change plays itself out contain the inevitability of change in their DNA.

OF COURSE, DIFFERENT INSTITUTIONS breed different conversations. Emerging institutions have fewer expectations, for example, than do older ones, which tend to have more defined ideas about what a building should be. "You have different conversations with different clients," says Packard. "Clients can be more open or closed."

A BREAKTHROUGH ATTITUDE FOR what a building might be, and how it would perform, emerged from this interrogatory process, and ZGF itself internalized both the attitude and the ideas emerging from discussions. The Port of Portland project, for example, led the firm toward sustainable design and urbanized interiors; it was a short step from the social ecosystem of the interior to the ecosystems of the urban and natural environments.

THE ARCHITECTS EVEN APPLIED the self-analytical process to their own facility. In the design of their downtown Portland offices, they performed a culture charrette on their own staff—with no partners allowed—and produced a mixed-use building, with apartments on the upper floors and their own offices on four lower floors, along with street-level retail and five levels of below-grade parking. The exploratory system of design opened communication within the office, which in turn was reified in the open studio environment with lounges and connecting stairs linking the four floors, explains Eugene Sandoval, another of ZGF's design partners.

Breaking Boundaries

INTERACTING WITH, AND LEARNING FROM, renowned thinkers in their fields, honing in on the culture of the institution, learning where the clients want to take that culture and how the building can support it—these are all approaches that inform ZGF's practice, even across building types. But the attitude and process have been most productive and innovative in the sciences. As disciplines break down, especially with the lingua franca of computational science, chemists are practicing physics, physicists are dabbling in biology, and biologists are taking on engineering. Advances in science are happening at the margins, outside of disciplines as they have been traditionally defined. "How can I break down barriers in architecture, and move it in a direction which responds to the breakdown in disciplines?" asks Frasca, who calls research buildings "the cathedrals of our times." Under this influence, the buildings are becoming fluid, beyond simple flexibility.

"**THE GREAT THING ABOUT WORKING** with these institutions is that there are no boundaries, they have no preconceptions," says Frasca. "They think about buildings as they think about science. You don't know in advance where the science is going to land. The same with a building for this kind of client: Not knowing is exciting. We work through images that evolve in the dialogue."

THE ARCHITECTS APPLY THEIR PROCESS of systematic open dialogue to building types beyond scientific research facilities. Hospitals, for example, have been a special venue of exploration in which the designers aim at bringing together not only the highly technical requirements of the building type, but also the community of disparate players, from medical staff and technicians to patients and their families.

WORKING AT THE CHILDREN'S HOSPITAL in Denver, ZGF found through its interview process that hospitals, like research facilities, should not just be free-standing architectural objects that are the sum total of programmatic requirements. Interviews and observation revealed various needs, especially in a hospital intended for children.

IN THE LONG HISTORY OF HOSPITAL EVOLUTION, clinical design that was, and looked, antiseptic might have been a major improvement over facilities dating from the 19th century. But ZGF found a whole body of new thinking directed at changing hospital culture. Especially in a children's hospital, there is a psychological imperative to creating spaces in which the family and kids can be together. Allocating space for a chair or bed right next to a premature baby allows a level of involvement that is helpful to both patient and family, and eases the transition to home care. The design of the workplace could also help to reduce staff stress.

MOREOVER, CONVERSATIONS INDICATED that children need dedicated places where they can socialize among their peers, including such venues as playrooms, teen lounges, and movie theaters. The hospital could and should be equipped with such casual amenities as basketball hoops, pool tables, and even telephone booths. To give the family a sense of both control over their environment and a sense of belonging, the facility should be as embracing as a hotel; for example, a suite with a shared kitchen and laundry room allows the family to live close to the child in an environment that approximates the reassuring routines of a home. Digital systems in hospital rooms even allow children to exercise some control in creating their own environments.

THE ABILITY TO APPLY EVIDENCE-BASED DESIGN principles to the hospital environment addresses research at a variety of levels with direct clinical outcomes. Within this family-oriented and patient-centered care facility, the design maximized natural light and connections to nature. The architects also experimented with color theory and the impact on the healing process. The environment could, at least partially, be curative.

ARCHITECTS OFTEN TALK ABOUT EDUCATING CLIENTS, assuming that they are the agents of enlightenment. But the originality of the ZGF position is that enlightenment lies in a process of mutual exploration sometimes led by the client. "Sometimes they're pushing us along," notes Mabe, "and that level of engagement sustains our creativity."

ONE OF ZGF'S MOST PRODUCTIVE RECENT DIALOGUES was with J. Craig Venter, a scientist famous not only for sequencing the human genome, but for achieving it in a random-access program. (The rival National Institutes of Health scientists preferred to stay in the box, and pursued their research in a more linear, sequential way.) When Venter interviewed ZGF about designing the J. Craig Venter Institute in La Jolla, California, he assumed his out-of-the-box attitude, and talked of building the Salk Institute of the 21st century, creating a highly flexible research building that would be as forward-looking today as the Salk was in its time.

CHIEF AMONG HIS REQUIREMENTS was a building with a zero carbon footprint, a green building that would exceed the highest LEED rating. Though linked into the grid, it could operate off the grid, like a self-sustaining organism. Venter wanted to green even the building process, using recycled construction materials. "Craig was saying in his own way that the Salk is the news of the 20th century, spawning generations of lab buildings, and he wanted to go beyond that to create the most sustainable building in the world," says Mabe.

CLIENT AND ARCHITECTS BEGAN with a series of conversations on the sustainability of mechanical systems. They reassessed what drives the interdependent air systems of the building—how heating, cooling, and purification components interface with each other and with natural ventilation. Sustainability became such an infectious goal that this new building caused the clients to rethink their own research process and culture.

THE DESIRE TO BUILD THE FAINTEST FOOTPRINT possible led the architects to structure the building in engineered wood rather than steel, a recycled composite material that led ZGF to think about the building in a totally different way. Besides the advantage of recycled wood over steel because of its lower embodied energy, Venter, a yachtsman, liked the image of a wood structure sailing through the landscape. For the long north façade, the architects designed a lamella system, which acts as a truss to resist lateral forces.

THE CLIMATE OF THOUGHT THAT SURROUNDED THE PROJECT invited innovation on all issues, including the apparently prosaic question of concrete. An engineer employed by the contractor brought a passel of jars with additives that could reduce the carbon footprint of concrete (which accounts for a disproportionate share of the world's total carbon emissions). The most promising jar contained slag, an abundant byproduct of iron smelting. Added to concrete, slag reacts chemically, significantly reducing carbon emission and incidentally turning the concrete into a warm charcoal color as it marbleizes the surface. The Salk Institute is famous for its refined texture and clarity. The concrete at the Venter Institute, when it is finished, promises to gain notoriety for reasons of its own.

A New Idealism

TURNING THE DESIGN PROCESS in on itself through a practice of observation and interviewing, the architects at ZGF have revisited and recast the fundamentals of design as a process of research, much of it oral. They have opened design beyond the assumption of good taste wrapped around an efficient plan. As Frasca says, "Buildings have purposes, not just function. They should not be formulaic; they are not reductive. It's about 'more' rather than 'less.' It's about responding to a culture, not just a setting. It's about what the building contributes, and what it takes." The architects at ZGF are pursuing a new idealism, looking not for an aesthetic monument but a response to a program predicated on continuous change.

IN A VERY BROAD SENSE, the architects are creating cultural environments, built within an orbit of concerns that includes everything from the physics of green to the conversational patterns of scientists drawn to elevator lobbies for the ride and scientific gossip. Taken to the optimal extreme, as in the Venter Institute, the architects are aiming at creating environmental organisms with changing patterns of pro-active behavior. The buildings are no longer passive receptacles, but shapers of values consciously posited in the design process and sustained over the life of the building. The result is not an unfeeling, bionic building that functions on its own, but one that behaves as a nearly natural organism programmed with cultural values.

BREAKING THE CONVENTIONAL PROCESS OF DESIGN, opening the system to admit non-traditional concerns, ZGF is pushing design into very promising architectural territory. The firm's synoptic practice expands the potential of what a building can be.

ONE

OBSERVATION

It is our belief that when buildings are based on preconceptions they are derivative of notions that came from another time and place and constrain the opportunity for discovery, invention, and relevance. Observation leads us to discover what is unique about a project. Observation is what breathes life into the program and its place.

University of California, San Diego

University of California, San Diego | Rebecca and John Moores UCSD Cancer Center | San Diego, California | The Cancer Center is structured to integrate clinical care, basic and translational research, cancer prevention, and administrative departments under one roof in a "bench-to-bedside" approach to conquering cancer. The ultimate design goal for this multi-purpose complex was to create a residential scale that facilitates a culture of interaction and patient-friendliness. The complex comprises a three-story clinical services and education facility and a five-story research building. The unifying base— a cancer commons and outdoor gardens for dining and interaction—provides a "living room" between the two buildings for staff, clinicians, and researchers to meet and exchange ideas. A tranquil bamboo courtyard outside the lobby and a series of smaller healing gardens offer relaxing settings for patients, their families, and staff.

A tranquil, shaded courtyard
serves as an extended lobby.
Large planters with bamboo and
other landscape materials create
intimate outdoor "rooms" where
patients and families can meet.

Zimmer Gunsul Frasca

Outside the laboratory environment, areas for both formal and informal gatherings are provided to encourage interaction among researchers.

A key goal of the cancer center is patient-focused care, as illustrated by the Infusion Center's Garden of Hope, a meditation room, and family waiting areas.

The Children's Hospital

The Children's Hospital | **Denver, Colorado** | From the outset, The Children's Hospital was designed to reflect the principles of family-centered care and evidence-based design, with the focus on patients and their families and how staff could best care for them. The result reflects the thought given to all factors that can influence healing: color, texture, natural light, art, access to the outdoors, and amenities ranging from hotel-like sleeping rooms for families to a teen center with a movie theater and gelato bar. The focal point of the building's interior is a central atrium that serves as the hospital's "living room." Other design goals included integrating the new hospital complex into the University of Colorado Health Sciences Center campus, and reflecting the Colorado landscape, geography, and culture.

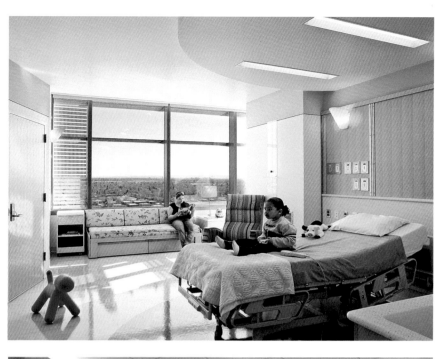

42

Future TenseFuture Tense

University of California, Berkeley

University of California, Berkeley | Stanley Hall | Berkeley, California | The new Stanley Hall creates space for programs at the intersection of biological and physical sciences and engineering, including the new Department of Bioengineering, and state-of-the-art computational laboratories. The 11-story facility (three below grade; eight above) is at the eastern gateway of the grand mall envisioned by John Galen Howard in the original master plan for the Berkeley campus. The building massing responds to the sloping site and the rich architectural context of the Hearst Mining Building and the Mining Circle. A five-story atrium forms the great room at the heart of the building and provides visual connections between researchers on multiple floors. A terrace café adjacent to the entry overlooks the Mining Circle.

The atrium and clerestory windows provide natural light and visual connection for the laboratories beyond.

The building's smaller scale façade facing Mining Circle is clad in Sierra white granite, the material used on the majority of the Beaux Arts buildings on campus. Its upper levels are partially clad in naturally weathered copper. Together, the materials help break the mass of the building and integrate it into the Berkeley campus.

Zimmer Gunsul Frasca

Perkins Coie, LLP

Perkins Coie, LLP | **Portland, Oregon** | A law firm comprising 80 lawyers and 50 support staff occupies three and a half floors at the top of a 10-story building in Portland's Pearl District. The modern office features refined detailing, an innovative palette of materials, and classic furnishings — a non-traditional design for the Northwest and, in particular, a law firm. Terrazzo floors, metal, glass, natural wood, and colored lacquer panels are the primary materials. An open stairway and translucent glass wall off the reception area extend to four levels and enhance communication among the staff.

CAPTAIN JOHN COUCH
ROOM

Three sizes of conference rooms
feature breakout spaces, erasable
glass panels, and tabletop
connectivity. Splashes of red on
lacquered walls provide visual
interest.

Zimmer Gunsul Frasca

Iowa State University

Iowa State University | Gerdin Business Building| Ames, Iowa | Located on the Central Lawn of Iowa State University, the limestone, brick, and glass Gerdin building is a modern complement to the historic buildings that surround it, creating a strong identity and presence for the School of Business. The facility houses lecture theaters, a multistory atrium, open stairs, lobbies, and common areas to encourage interaction between students and faculty in and out of the classroom.

Zimmer Gunsul Frasca

Ray Quinney & Nebeker, PC

Ray Quinney & Nebeker, PC | Salt Lake City, Utah | A 60-year-old law firm sought to revamp the interiors of its office in a move aimed at attracting and retaining young attorneys in a competitive market. The design is fresh and updated, while respecting the traditional heritage of the firm. It reconciles the contrasting styles by using cherry wood, stone, bamboo flooring, glass, and other conventional materials with modern detailing. The primary lobby and conferencing space is open and expansive to capture views of the Wasatch Mountain range.

University of California, Riverside

**University of California, Riverside | Entomology Building |
Riverside, California** | UC Riverside is internationally known for its
research programs in biological control, integrated pest management, and exotic insects. A replacement facility to provide offices
and modern laboratories for these research programs was sited
adjacent to one of the oldest buildings on campus. Following the
imperative that the new building complement its historic neighbor,
the three-level building is designed as two wings, each comprising
four faculty offices and four laboratory suites per level. The lowest
level of the east wing takes advantage of the sloped site by incorporating partially below-grade administrative offices, conference
facilities, and a sheltered, open courtyard. The two wings are linked
on the southwest corner by a vertical circulation element with a
curving glass enclosure. This signature design feature internally
facilitates interaction among occupants of the various laboratories
by drawing them into a unified series of common areas.

Zimmer Gunsul Frasca

Both the first- and second-level entrances of the building open directly into common areas, which house departmental exhibits, graduate student offices, and other shared facilities. Windows feature coated frits for exposures especially vulnerable to heat gain and glare.

Zimmer Gunsul Frasca

Ronald Reagan Federal Building

Ronald Reagan Federal Building and U.S. Courthouse | Santa Ana, California |
The 10-story Federal Building and U.S. Courthouse in Santa Ana serves the U.S. District Court, U.S. Bankruptcy Court, and related agencies. The linear site links the historic downtown of Santa Ana with a 1960s civic center. The building's exterior and portions of the interior public lobby and galleries are clad in two colors of travertine. Entrance pavilions on the south and north sides accommodate roof terraces. A long, narrow eight-story tower above the two-story base echoes the scale of the historic buildings near the site. Public lobbies on each of the courtroom floors look out over the city and the ocean beyond. Judges' chambers are accessed from a secure corridor that connects to each courtroom from behind the bench.

The light-colored travertine on both the exterior and interior celebrates the warm climate and light of southern California. The courtroom design references tradition while incorporating new technology.

TWO

COLLABORATION

The popular conception of the architect is that buildings spring from the brow of a single individual. Although it is true that the initiator and keeper of the soul of the project resides with one person, the complexity of a modern building and how it operates requires a broad range of experience and talent that cannot reside in a single individual. Our projects are shaped in important ways by a team within our office, by our clients, and by specialized consultants that enable us to make buildings that exceed all expectations.

Carnegie Institution

Carnegie Institution | Maxine F. Singer Building | Baltimore, Maryland | The new home of the Carnegie Institution's Department of Embryology is located adjacent to the Homewood Campus of The Johns Hopkins University. The building contains biochemistry laboratories suitable for cell and developmental genetics research and state-of-the-art genomic research, as well as core facilities and public areas for meetings and seminars. The building plan is a pinwheel, with the primary interaction space and auditorium at the center. Each research wing penetrates the surrounding forest and provides views to the creek and the neighborhoods beyond. Scientists' offices are virtually within the laboratories, with visual communication further enhanced through views, as well as of the outside, between offices in adjacent laboratory wings.

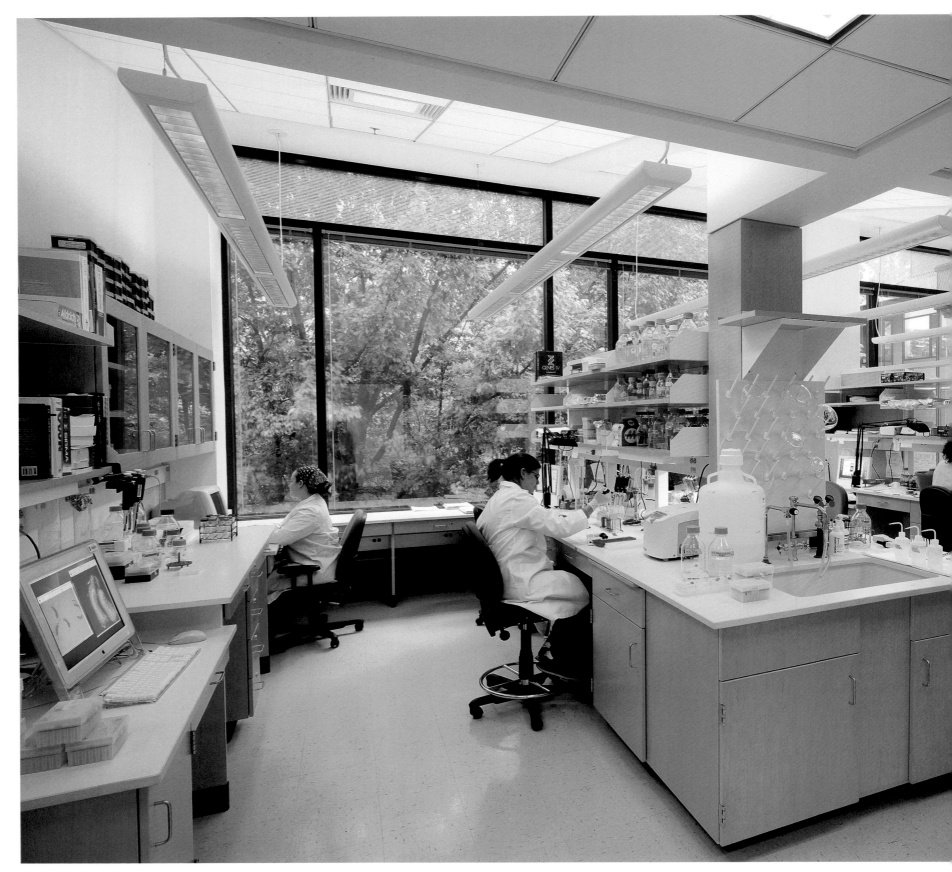

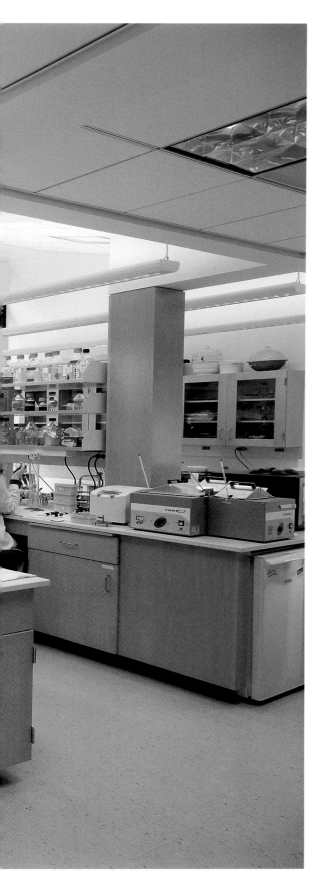

Although the laboratories are highly flexible, other spaces are specifically crafted to enhance their purpose and take advantage of their surroundings.

Future Tense

The exterior materials of brick, copper shingles, and glass relate to the Hopkins campus and easily integrate with the elements of nature that envelop the architecture on two sides.

U.S. Consulate Compound

U.S. Consulate Compound | **Istanbul, Turkey** | The U.S. Consulate in Istanbul is intended to provide a safe workplace for visitors and staff while representing the United States in a dignified manner to the host country. Built on a hill in a suburban community with magnificent views of the Bosphorus, the planning concept organizes the various departments around a central courtyard, allowing the occupants to enjoy the outdoors in a secure environment. The cafeteria with adjacent terraces offers prime views of the surroundings. A local travertine, a common building material in the region, is the principal exterior building skin.

Zimmer Gunsul Frasca

A two-story cafeteria off the courtyard is shared by the building occupants by day and also functions as a more formal entertaining space. Materials and design elements draw from the rich traditions of the host country.

Washington State University | **Vancouver Campus** | **Vancouver, Washington** | Over the last decade, ZGF has worked with WSU Vancouver to develop a 20-year master plan for a new 351-acre campus, followed by the programming and design of three phases of campus landscape and infrastructure projects, as well as a dozen structures. Program elements have included classrooms, offices, auditorium and conference space, teaching laboratories, a library, research facilities, food service, parking, and site improvements. Significant attention was paid to crafting open spaces that create a memorable campus identity tied to the natural features of the site, as well as internal spaces that make commuting students feel at home on the campus.

The master plan sets the campus
on an axis of symmetry that
provides spectacular views of two
volcanic peaks in the Cascade
Range: Mount Hood and Mount
St. Helens.

Zimmer Gunsul Frasca

Fred Hutchinson Cancer Research Center | **Seattle, Washington** | The world-renowned Fred Hutchinson Cancer Research Center in the late 1980s made the decision to consolidate its four divisions—Basic Sciences, Human Biology, Clinical Research, and Public Health Sciences—from a dozen disparate buildings near downtown Seattle. The resulting 14.3-acre Lake Union shoreline campus encompasses more than 1 million square feet of building space, including the Weintraub Basic Sciences Building, the E. Donnall Thomas Clinical Research Facility, the Seattle Cancer Care Alliance, the Yale Administration Building, and, most recently, the Robert M. Arnold Public Health Sciences Building. The campus, constructed in five phases to date, was master-planned to function as complete at each phase.

Zimmer Gunsul Frasca

Zimmer Gunsul Frasca

University of Michigan

University of Michigan | **Ann and Robert H. Lurie Biomedical Engineering Building Addition** | **Ann Arbor, Michigan** | Situated in a pivotal location on the north campus, the Ann and Robert H. Lurie Biomedical Engineering Building acts as a gateway to the entire College of Engineering. The new addition, with both renovated space and new construction, contains undergraduate classrooms, research laboratories, and offices to support new and expanded programs emphasizing cellular and molecular biotechnologies. The project provides a focus for faculty and researchers across the campus, creating an environment that enhances work at the highest level. The atrium interaction space is a key ingredient, fostering communication and interaction among faculty, visiting researchers, administrators, and students.

Zimmer Gunsul Frasca

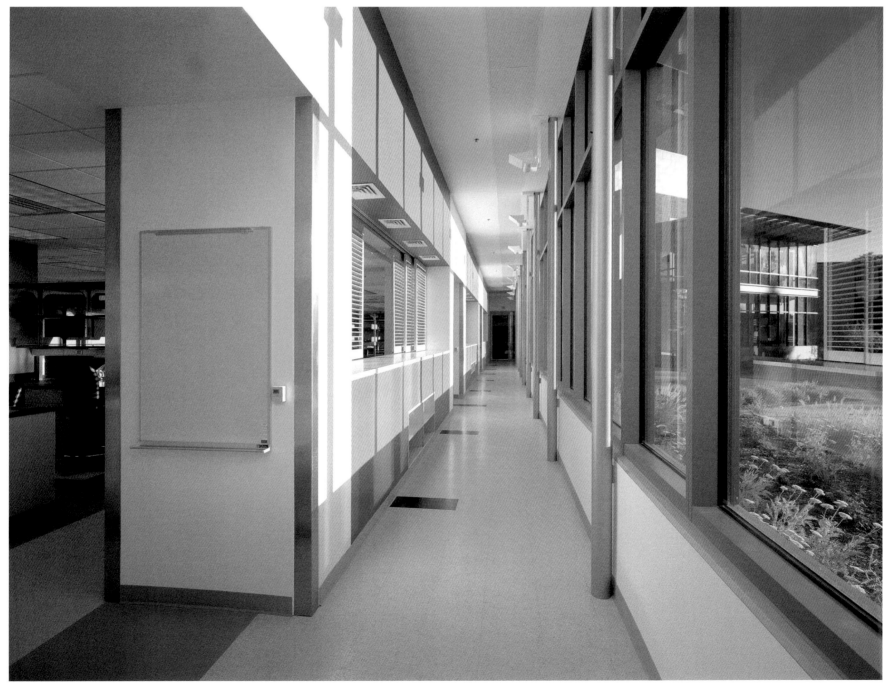

University of California, San Diego | **Leichtag Family Foundation Biomedical Research Building** | **San Diego, California** | The Leichtag building extends the existing research complex along the major drive of the UC San Diego central campus. Daylight is a key ingredient in this building, as a windowed atrium unites the five laboratory and office floors. A dichroic glass sculpture by artist Ed Carpenter intervenes at all levels of the atrium. Researchers can enjoy views of the newly created School of Medicine quad from exterior walkways along each floor, while strategically located common activity spaces encourage interaction. The building provides wet bench research laboratories, core facilities, support space, offices, and a 100-seat conference center that faces the new quad.

Zimmer Gunsul Frasca

Future Tense

San Diego's mild climate allows for exterior circulation, which maximizes flexibility and building efficiency. The core facilities and offices are located strategically at the ends of the open laboratories.

Safeco Insurance Companies

Safeco Insurance | **Redmond Campus Expansion** | **Redmond, Washington** | The master plan and expansion of Safeco's 46-acre headquarters addressed the phased development of an integrated campus of office buildings, cafeterias, conference areas, and service facilities. The plan separates pedestrian and vehicular circulation and incorporates a central greenway. A series of pathways connects seven new and existing buildings to create a natural, collegial, and interactive environment. Completed phases resulted in two three-story office buildings designed to maximize daylight and views to the outdoors, with a flexible, open office plan, along with parking, data center, 500-seat cafeteria, and adjacent conference center. The campus has since been acquired by Microsoft Corporation and ZGF is adapting it to meet their requirements.

At the heart of the campus green
is the cafeteria, which features tall
glass doors leading to an outdoor
dining terrace and reflecting pool.

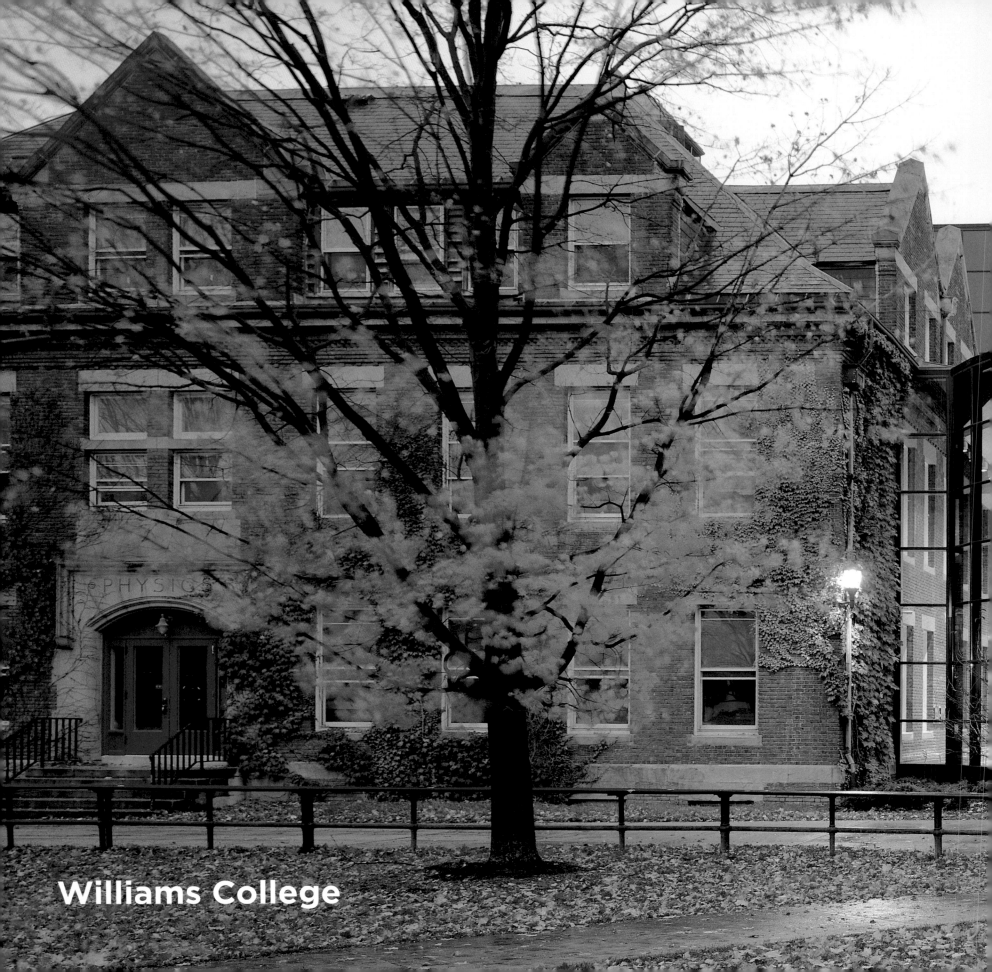

Williams College

Williams College | **The Science Center and Schow Science Library** | **Williamstown, Massachusetts** | The Science Center encompasses four existing buildings on the principal quad of the Williams College campus. A glass-enclosed café serves as a quiet intervention from the quad and creates a new entrance to what is now an interdisciplinary science complex. Three 1900s science buildings were renovated for dry laboratories, offices, conference rooms, and classrooms. Modern wet laboratories are located in a new wing to the south. The space between the old and new buildings was transformed into the sky-lit science library, which becomes the interior focus of the new complex.

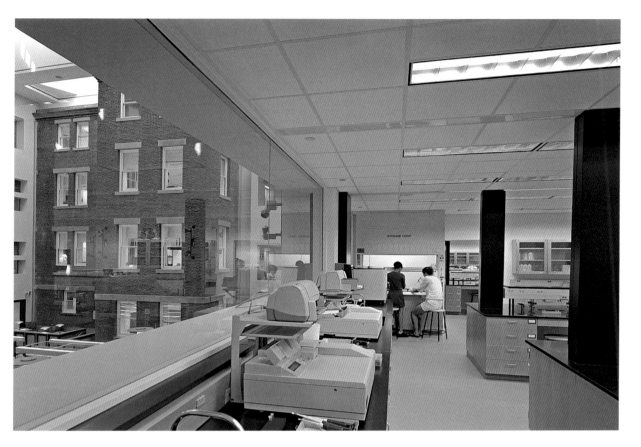

THREE

INTELLIGENCE

Intelligence follows observation and leads to invention. We research how things are being done now, and imagine how they could be done better in the future. The quest for sustainable design is one example. Builders throughout history have used the climate in intelligent ways to make buildings in harmony with the elements. As we continue to use this knowledge in design, we add to a building's sustainability by inventing and applying new technologies in ways not previously imagined.

Legacy Salmon Creek Hospital

Legacy Salmon Creek Hospital | Vancouver, Washington | A new 220-bed hospital and medical center built from "whole cloth" afforded the opportunity to create a patient-friendly, family-centered complex while attending to the state-of-the-art requirements of the medical staff. The 25-acre complex features a two-level entry with bridges from the parking structure into the second-level hospital lobby. Two outpatient clinics adjoined by an atrium connect into the same second-level circulation system. Amenities include a roof terrace with chapel, cafeteria with outdoor dining, and a garden at the entry drive designed for group gatherings as well as private meditation.

Zimmer Gunsul Frasca

Family waiting areas are located adjacent to the visitor elevator core and central to the patient rooms. Each patient room takes advantage of the predominantly southern view over a forested area and is fitted with sitting/sleeping accommodations for family members.

A clear, definable circulation system orients patients, staff, and visitors upon entry to the complex. The primary view of the hospital features a curved façade with large punched windows into the patient rooms and treatment spaces. *Loowit*, a sculpture by artist Lee Kelly, rises boldly from the lawn.

Zimmer Gunsul Frasca

University of California, Santa Barbara

University of California, Santa Barbara | Donald Bren School of Environmental Science and Management and Marine Sciences Building |
Santa Barbara, California | These two buildings were designed in tandem but constructed in phases on the last ocean-front site available on the UC Santa Barbara campus. Their forms mediate between the campus and their coastal location, taking advantage of the unique climate and views. Both buildings include teaching and research laboratories, faculty and departmental offices, conference facilities, and support areas. Serving as a role model for environmental stewardship, the Bren School was one of the first 12 buildings in the country to become LEED certified and the first research laboratory to be Platinum-certified. The Marine Sciences Building is also LEED certified. Open courtyards unite the laboratory wing and the office wing in each building, while upper-level walkways provide access to offices as well as spaces for planned and spontaneous interdepartmental interactions.

Entry portals serve as gateways to each building's central courtyard. Open walkways increase visibility between floors and encourage informal interaction.

Pacific Lutheran University

Pacific Lutheran University | **Morken Center for Learning and Technology** | **Tacoma, Washington** | The Morken Center combines three traditionally unrelated departments at Pacific Lutheran University: the School of Business, the Department of Computer Science and Computer Engineering, and the Department of Mathematics. It also unifies a previously bifurcated institution with a central "lawn" and a new University entrance. The academic facility includes classrooms, laboratories, faculty offices, conference rooms, and a central commons and garden. The Morken Center is constructed with a palette of materials familiar to the campus. However, its modest aesthetic belies a building technology and an academic configuration that is uniquely flexible. Its recognitions include a LEED Gold rating.

The completed center opens up a new area of campus, provides a second primary entry, and accommodates a synthesis of usually unrelated graduate and undergraduate programs.

The center's two wings are joined by a two-story lobby with common spaces intended to promote informal exchanges between a new mix of disciplines.

Zimmer Gunsul Frasca

Duke University

Duke University | **Fitzpatrick Center for Interdisciplinary Engineering, Medicine, and Applied Sciences** | **Durham, North Carolina** | The master plan for the Duke campus mandates that all buildings in the zone adjacent to the original campus adhere in both scale and materials to its predecessors. The center for the Pratt School of Engineering and the Duke School of Medicine was built to house research and teaching activities for the school's three strategic initiatives: Bioengineering, Photonics, and Communications; Materials Science; and Materials Engineering. The building carefully weaves into the landscape and makes a crucial connection to the central campus while creating a new focal point to existing engineering buildings. A clean room, characterization lab, and testing facility are also shared with Duke's Trinity College of Arts and Sciences.

Zimmer Gunsul Frasca

The program included 19th-century rooms for casual interaction as well as 21st-century spaces where technology was the driving force of design.

An atrium with a connecting stairway provides the principal interaction space bridging the three levels of the building.

Oregon Health & Science University

Oregon Health & Science University | **Biomedical Research Building** | **Portland, Oregon** | OHSU required a world-class facility that would add to its research complex and continue to attract and retain scientists involved in biomedical and translational research. The new building connects with a family of four others to maximize flexibility and interaction. Common facilities, such as a library and large meeting areas, are at the end of the chain, to be easily shared with the adjacent buildings. Offices and large interaction areas are grouped together adjacent to the open laboratories, which can be readily reconfigured and customized to meet the needs of evolving research teams. Taking advantage of the steep slope of the site, an Advanced Imaging Research Center is located below grade but accessed from the courtyard level to facilitate connections to the outpatient clinic. Energy efficiency was a major driver of the building design. The building incorporates sustainable features in multiple areas, including the building envelope, the HVAC system, and stormwater management and has achieved LEED Silver certification.

Outdoor terraces adjacent to the
common areas bring visual relief to
the highly specialized interiors.

The building interiors are designed
to take maximum advantage of
the spectacular views.

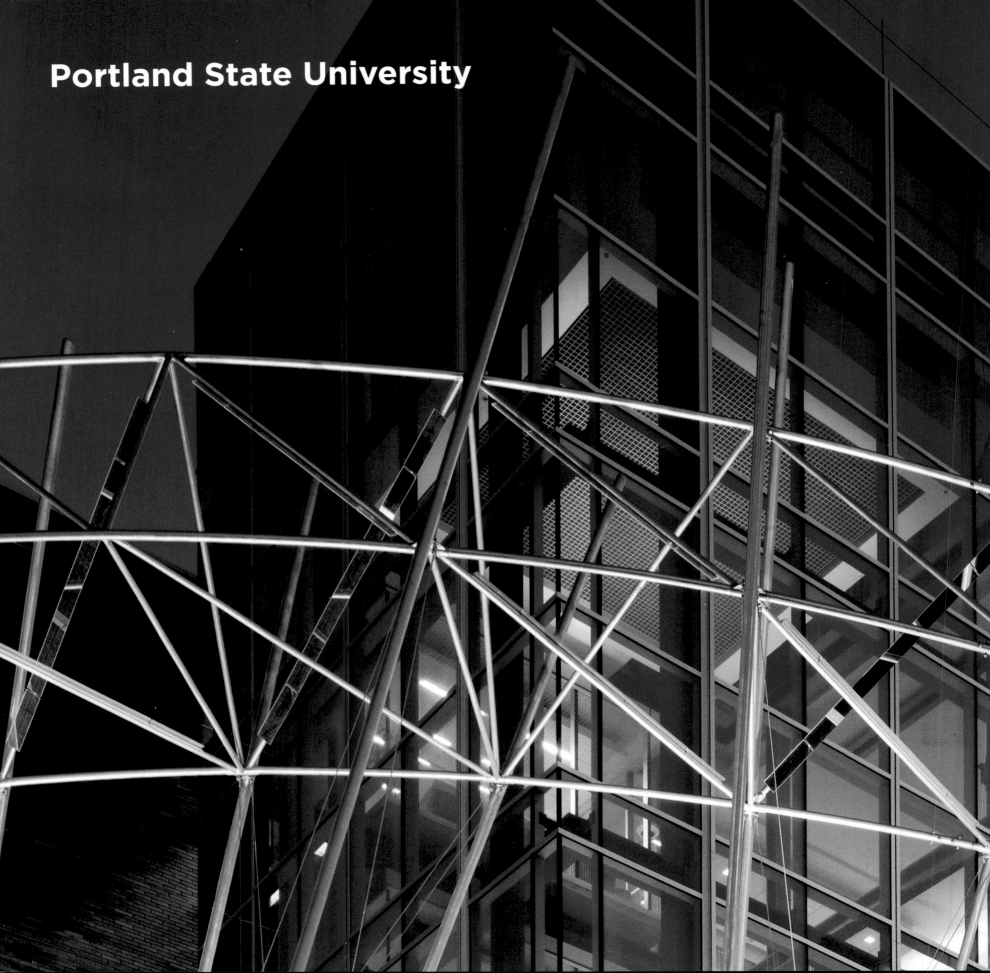

Portland State University

FARIBORZ M
COLLEGE OF
& COMPUTE

Portland State University | **Northwest Center for Engineering, Science and Technology** | **Portland, Oregon** | This research and teaching building houses civil, mechanical engineering, and systems engineering programs for Portland State University's College of Engineering & Computer Science. Located in an existing urban renewal area adjacent to downtown Portland, it forms the eastern edge of the university. The five above-grade stories include classrooms, laboratories, a 120-seat lecture auditorium, student services office, and offices of the Dean of the College. Three below-grade stories contain a parking garage and additional offices. The building, which incorporates sustainable design features, such as a geothermal heat exchange system, achieved a LEED Gold certification.

The building itself is designed to be a teaching tool for engineering students. Exposed structure and accessible building systems are only some of the elements that allow for this.

U.S. Environmental Protection Agency

U.S. Environmental Protection Agency | **Region 8 Headquarters** | **Denver, Colorado** | Located on an urban brownfield site adjacent to downtown Denver's Union Station, the EPA Region 8 Headquarters is the result of a design process that sought to integrate a contemporary, high-performance, secure, and environmentally sensitive building into one of Denver's most important historic and civic districts. A key program goal was to establish the building as an architectural and sustainable design landmark that embodies the EPA's mission to protect and enhance human health and the environment. The result is a nine-story, LEED Gold-certified building that sets an example of environmental stewardship, with features that include Denver's first green roof designed to treat and manage stormwater.

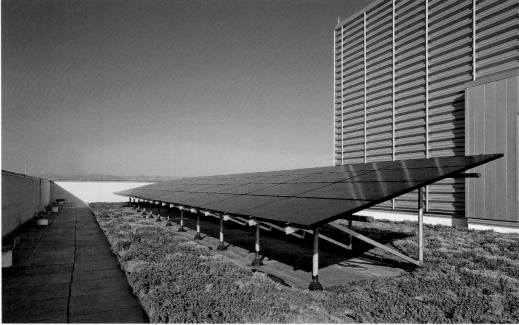

Photovoltaic panels on the
building's green roof are dedicated
to the emergency power supply.
The eco-roof is populated with
a native, drought-tolerant plant
species.

Zimmer Gunsul Frasca

FOUR

CULTURE

The traditions of our clients and the places they inhabit have been central to our work throughout the half century of our practice. We have always immersed ourselves in the cultures of our clients, envisioning where they want to take their organizations and how the design of the building can best support their goals.

U.S. Food and Drug Administration

U.S. Food and Drug Administration | FDA at Irvine, Regional Laboratory and District Office | Irvine, California | FDA at Irvine culminates the agency's strategic plan to consolidate 18 aging analytical laboratories into five multipurpose and four specialty laboratories. The facility is sited on an irregularly shaped, 10-acre site overlooking a marshy wetland of upper Newport Bay. The geometry of the building's plan closely marries site considerations with strict functional requirements. The curved shape of the building embraces the native wetland and draws the landscape directly up to its base. Three two-story rectangular laboratory blocks are arranged in a stepped echelon facing southwest. The office components of the program are attached directly to the laboratories, with glass walls separating the two elements. Stretching from the entrance lobby to the library at its far end, a two-story circulation spine is conceived as a curved internal street, in the California tradition of uniting indoors and outdoors. Through its openness, the building reveals the intent of the FDA to build a newly integrated work culture.

Zimmer Gunsul Frasca

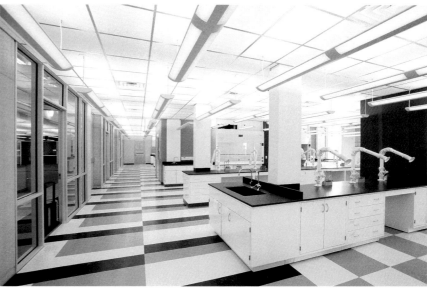

Concrete walls serve as both structure and finish and combine with perforated, corrugated copper panels and stainless-steel sunshades to protect the building's southern façade. The curved north wall dramatically denotes the building's entrance.

Cornell University

Cornell University | Duffield Hall Nanotechnology Research Facility | Ithaca, New York | The engineering quad of the Cornell campus is surrounded by post-World War II buildings that intermittently connect with one another and provide an interactive environment, a fundamental concept to teaching and research. Duffield Hall, which engages the electrical engineering building directly, forms an atrium with interaction, study, and food-service spaces that creates a focus for faculty and student life. The research spaces contain highly specialized nanofabrication, nanocharacterization, materials growth, and nanobiotechnology laboratories, with attendant faculty offices and conference rooms. A colloquium room that projects out over the quad offers magnificent views of the main campus and surrounding landscape.

Beyond all the technological aspects of the building, the new atrium (connecting Phillips, Duffield, and Upson Halls) is equipped with study alcoves, collaboration spaces, and dining facilities to encourage "intellectual collisions" outside the laboratory environment.

Dr. Donald and Beret Mott Children's Center

Dr. Donald and Beret Mott Children's Center | **Puyallup, Washington** | Natural patterns, lively colors, and integrated art installations create a comfortable patient-centered setting for patients and families who visit this children's therapy unit. Designed to support multidisciplinary care for physically and developmentally disabled children, the facility offers specialty services such as physical therapy, assistive technology, orthotic intervention, computer technology, psychology, and speech-language therapy. Ark and ocean imagery permeates the design inside and out as illustrated by curved, horizontal cedar siding, round windows, wavy landscaped paths, and a conch-shaped therapy pool bathed in natural light.

Zimmer Gunsul Frasca

The metaphor of the ark is brought to life through playful design features including "porthole" windows, colorful murals depicting sea life, and a variety of other natural motifs.

Microsoft Cafeteria

Microsoft Cafeteria | Redmond, Washington | ZGF's long-standing working relationship with Microsoft Corporation began with the master plan and design of a new campus in Redmond, Washington. Since then, more than 1 million square feet of office, research and development, conference, support, and parking space have been designed on the company's original Redmond campus. In all cases, the focus has been on creating high-quality, flexible work environments that enhance the company's business objectives within a natural landscape. The cafeteria shown here is part of a three-building office complex on the Redmond campus.

Zimmer Gunsul Frasca Architects

Zimmer Gunsul Frasca Architects | **Los Angeles, California** | The relocation of ZGF's Los Angeles office presented the opportunity to unite the staff in a workplace reflecting the ideals of environmental responsibility and community building. The 37th floor of a downtown high-rise was chosen for its high ceilings, 13-foot-tall windows, and few structural obstacles. Beginning with the loft warehouse concept, the space features the industrial look of exposed ceilings above open plan studios, but adds a dropped ceiling plane to reduce the scale of the space over reception, conference, and meeting rooms. The design juxtaposes raw and industrial elements with warm woods and bright colors. Systems are subdivided into smaller neighborhoods so the space functions as a community, much like an urban environment.

Open, flexible workstations and shelving on wheels encourage teamwork. The elliptical cutouts in the dropped ceiling reveal colorful coves that add a sense of playfulness to the entire office.

The Eliot Tower

The Eliot Tower | Portland, Oregon | The Eliot Tower is an 18-story, 225-unit residential condominium tower and plaza in Portland's growing West End district. Overlooked for decades, this urban neighborhood is developing a residential and retail environment that is integrating an historic collection of diverse institutions (libraries, fine and performing arts centers, and places of worship and education). The Eliot has proved a conspicuous catalyst for this social, economic, and cultural reformation.

The transparency of the building skin
exposes life within while connecting
the building's occupants to their city.

Zimmer Gunsul Frasca

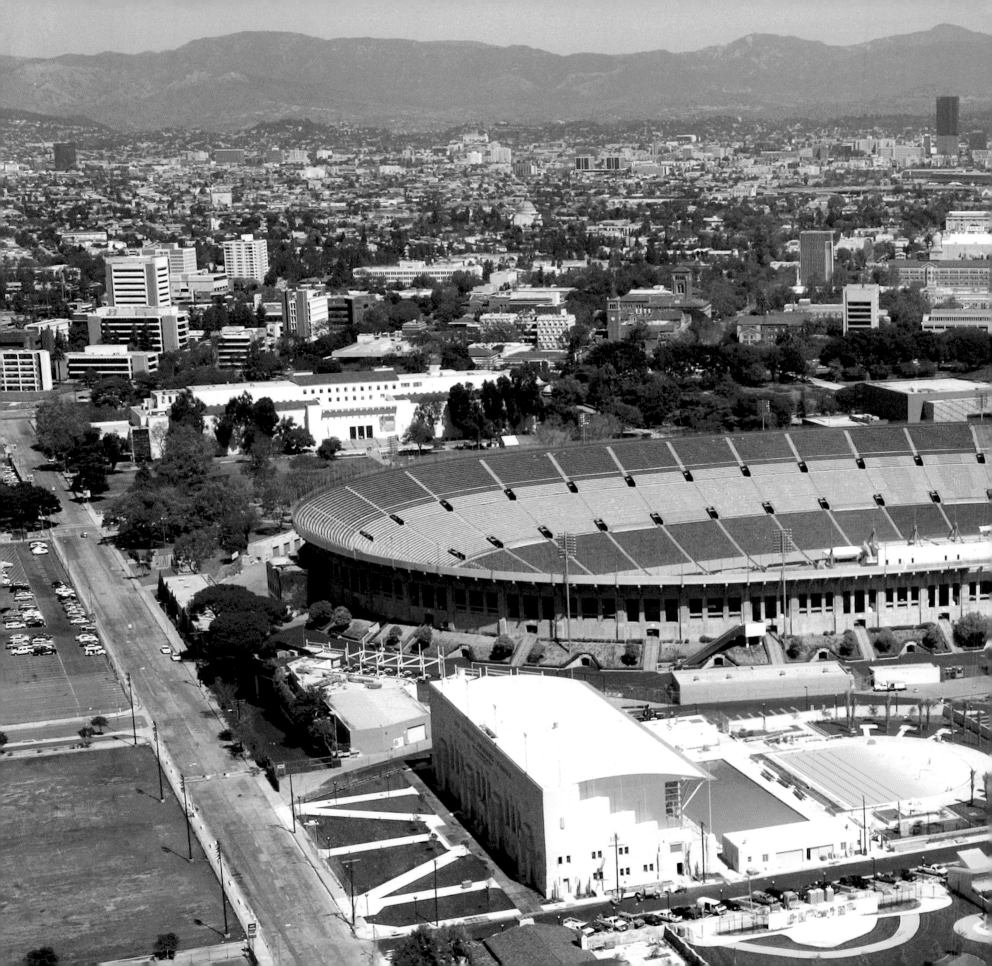

Exposition Park

Exposition Park Intergenerational Community Center | John C. Argue Swim Stadium | Los Angeles, California | An idea for a prototypical recreational complex sprang from the plan to recover Exposition Park from years of neglect. The Exposition Park Intergenerational Community Center, located on a six-acre site, comprises three separate facilities—all intended to encourage cross-generational interaction. In addition to new child care and newly restored senior centers, the 1932 Olympic Swimming Stadium was renovated and expanded to include basketball courts, meeting rooms, an auditorium, and exercise and locker rooms, while maintaining its original purpose as an aquatic center. A new three-story building inserted within the footprint, and reuse of three original walls of the historic structure, saved the stadium from complete demolition. One thousand of the original bleacher seats were retained, and the swimming pools were restored. The new portion of the building is contemporary yet respectful of the building's historic Art Deco façade.

The contemporary steel-and-glass structure rises above the original building. Just as the architecture harmonizes old and new, so does the facility's function—uniting people of all ages as they celebrate community.

Zimmer Gunsul Frasca

Science Center of Iowa

Science Center of Iowa & Blank IMAX® DomeTheater | **Des Moines, Iowa** | Located in the heart of Des Moines and visible from the riverfront, the Science Center of Iowa is one of a series of new buildings that have contributed to the transformation of downtown. A museum and learning center are sheathed in terra cotta, polished stainless-steel panels, glass, and a contrasting yellow brick. The museum features hands-on exhibits located in six dynamic "experience platforms," a 220-seat IMAX® theater, the 50-seat domed Star Theater, and the Science Adventure Theater for live performances. The Iowa Learning Center offers educational programs, a resource center, and cyberlabs used by local teachers and students to complement school curricula and enhance content within the exhibit areas of the museum.

The architectural expression of the Science Center is crafted to "engage and inspire." Covered with polished stainless steel panels, the IMAX® Dome Theater is animated by a surrounding reflecting pool, illuminated both day and night.

Experience Platforms
John Deere Adventure Theater
Principal Hall
Elevator

The Science Center of Iowa
Meredith Family Center for Creative Learning

Small Discoveries
Who Are We?
Science Is Where You Find It

Glass-enclosed stairs positioned at both ends of the north façade resemble lanterns when illuminated at night, serving as a beacon from various points in the city.

National Institutes of Health

National Institutes of Health | **Mark O. Hatfield Clinical Research Center** | **Bethesda, Maryland** | The 200-acre Bethesda campus of the National Institutes of Health is a world center of translational research. ZGF won an international competition resulting in a major addition and modernization of the complex, which was built in the late 1940s and expanded intermittently. The new facility integrates a 250-bed hospital with research laboratories conveniently connected by an interaction space for physicians and researchers. This seven-story science court, adjacent to two outdoor courtyards, is the physical heart of the expanded complex. It provides interaction space on each level. Interstitial spaces maximize flexibility of building systems, allowing laboratories to be converted to beds or vice versa.

As well as providing for its own specific requirements, the addition was intended to re-order what is now a 4 million-square-foot building complex. Exterior views from circulation elements provide necessary clarity.

Zimmer Gunsul Frasca

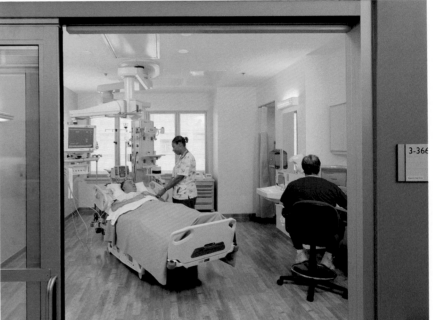

For future flexibility, the high-function laboratories and patient rooms were designed to be interchangeable.

FIVE

INVENTION

Invention in building should not be for its own sake but as a result of addressing issues particular to a program, a climate, or a place. It can be about the arrangement of spaces on a site, a way to minimize the carbon footprint, or how a particular building component is crafted. Relevant invention happens only after rigorous observation and collaboration.

Portland International Airport

Portland International Airport | Terminal Expansion | Portland, Oregon | Like most airports, Portland International has expanded by accretion over the last 50 years to accommodate increased air traffic and evolving security requirements. ZGF, which was involved in the initial expansion more than 40 years ago, has completed a 10-year expansion of the north and south terminals, with the primary goal of ease and clarity for the passenger. A glass canopy and two serpentine pedestrian bridges over the enplaning road connect the vertical circulation of the parking structure and main terminal, providing weather-protected access to the terminal from auto or public transportation. Portland's light rail system connects from the terminal's interior to the downtown and surrounding metropolitan area. Active retail centers are located on both sides of security zones; generous concourse lobbies at both the north and south ends of the terminal contain additional retail and expanded security stations.

Zimmer Gunsul Frasca

Concourse lobbies at the north and south ends of the terminal allow generous space for security. Within the concourses, nodal areas contain retail and food vendors that serve adjacent gates.

University of Arizona

University of Arizona | Thomas W. Keating Bioresearch Building and Medical Research Building | Tucson, Arizona | The two research buildings support faculty and students from multiple disciplines, other institutions, and industry partners to more easily translate basic research findings into real-world applications. The buildings are physically linked by enclosed walkways, a shared courtyard, and a 90-foot-tall metal Ramada structure to foster interaction and allow researchers to share core research facilities, equipment, and meeting rooms. Both buildings are designed as four levels of flexible, interdisciplinary laboratories, faculty offices, graduate student workstations, and conference spaces organized into research neighborhoods. One of the most important design decisions was to locate office and meeting areas near, but not inside, the laboratories. Conference rooms and informal gathering spaces are scattered throughout each floor and outdoors to stimulate interaction.

Faculty and students from multiple departments have offices grouped together in research neighborhoods. Formal and informal gathering spaces on each floor encourage interaction; connecting stairways further enhance communication.

University of Arizona

University of Arizona | Chemical Sciences Building | Tucson, Arizona | This research building, located in the historic campus core, was designed to reduce its scale in relation to adjacent chemistry and science buildings. It is organized by its two distinct types of space, laboratories and offices. Large glass windows in the building's east lobby and interaction spaces penetrate a curving, corrugated copper wall that frames an enhanced landscaped plaza. The west elevation is also screened by a perforated, corrugated copper wall, which protects the exterior stair and acts as a backdrop to an adjacent outdoor garden. A glass curtain wall takes advantage of the north orientation, where all offices are located, and contrasts with, while reflecting, the brick façade of the Chemistry Building. Pedestrian bridges, with glass and metal panels, connect to existing buildings.

Conference room windows are
screened by a curving wall of
perforated copper. In the corridors
between the laboratories and
offices, informal gathering
spaces with white boards invite
spontaneous discussion.

The offices along the building's
north elevation face the existing
Chemistry Building and overlook
the tree-shaded Magic Alley.

Fourth & Madison Tower

Fourth & Madison Tower | **Seattle, Washington** | The 40-story Fourth & Madison Tower is one of the first buildings to reform the skyline of 21st-century Seattle. The mixed-use development provides retail, parking, and office space in an elegant silhouette. Sheathed in light-colored granite, metal, and glass, the building evokes a modern expression that distinguishes it from neighbors in the heart of the city's financial district. The highly energy-efficient tower maximizes daylight and provides 360-degree views of Puget Sound and the mountains beyond.

The building lobby features a four-story atrium enlivened by retail and a custom art installation by James Carpenter consisting of narrow glass fins coated with dichroic film. A roof terrace on the seventh floor comprises a large garden bordered by smaller, intimate spaces and a children's play area.

San Diego State University

San Diego State University | **Transit Center** | **San Diego, California** | This underground station is part of the new 5.5-mile Mission Valley East light rail alignment. The project places regional light rail services at the very heart of San Diego State University, while simultaneously enhancing open space, pedestrian connections, and campus community redevelopment. The facility links three levels of circulation: the bus transit center on Aztec Walk, a major pedestrian boulevard; the mezzanine bridge 20 feet below grade; and the tunnel trolley station platform located 50 feet below. Adjacent green space slopes down to the mezzanine level to allow for clerestory windows to bring daylight into the tunnel station platform.

Zimmer Gunsul Frasca

The 220-foot tied-arch pedestrian bridge that crosses College Avenue connects the station to the east campus housing district.

Zimmer Gunsul Frasca

By sloping the adjacent green space, the design places one side of the station platform at grade, allowing natural daylight to fill the tunnel. Hanging sculptures made of thin, stainless steel cable wires animate the station's interior, undulating in the wind generated as trains approach.

Memorial Sloan-Kettering Cancer Center

Memorial Sloan-Kettering Cancer Center | The Mortimer B. Zuckerman Research Center | New York, New York | The design for The Mortimer B. Zuckerman Research Center, located on a narrow site on Memorial Sloan-Kettering's Manhattan campus, is intended to lead the institution into the 21st century by providing not only a symbolic center for the campus but an exemplary environment to support the facility's research mission. The project is being built in two phases. The first is a 21-story research tower that contains wet and core laboratory programs. A glass-enclosed communicating stair, with adjacent conference and lounge space at each level, creates a focal point for interaction for the entire building. Phase two will incorporate computational biology and graduate school programs, as well as a 350-seat auditorium and conference center. The project is on track to receive LEED certification.

Zimmer Gunsul Frasca

Movable desks and laboratory benches can adapt quickly to shifts in number of researchers and their protocols. Generous 9$\frac{1}{2}$-foot-high ceilings in laboratories provide further flexibility in equipping these areas.

Meeting and interaction rooms are located next to offices and across an open corridor from the interaction staircase, designed to foster encounters among researchers. Original artwork integrated into the glass is unique to each floor.

The cybercafé, located on the ground floor, serves researchers from the entire building.

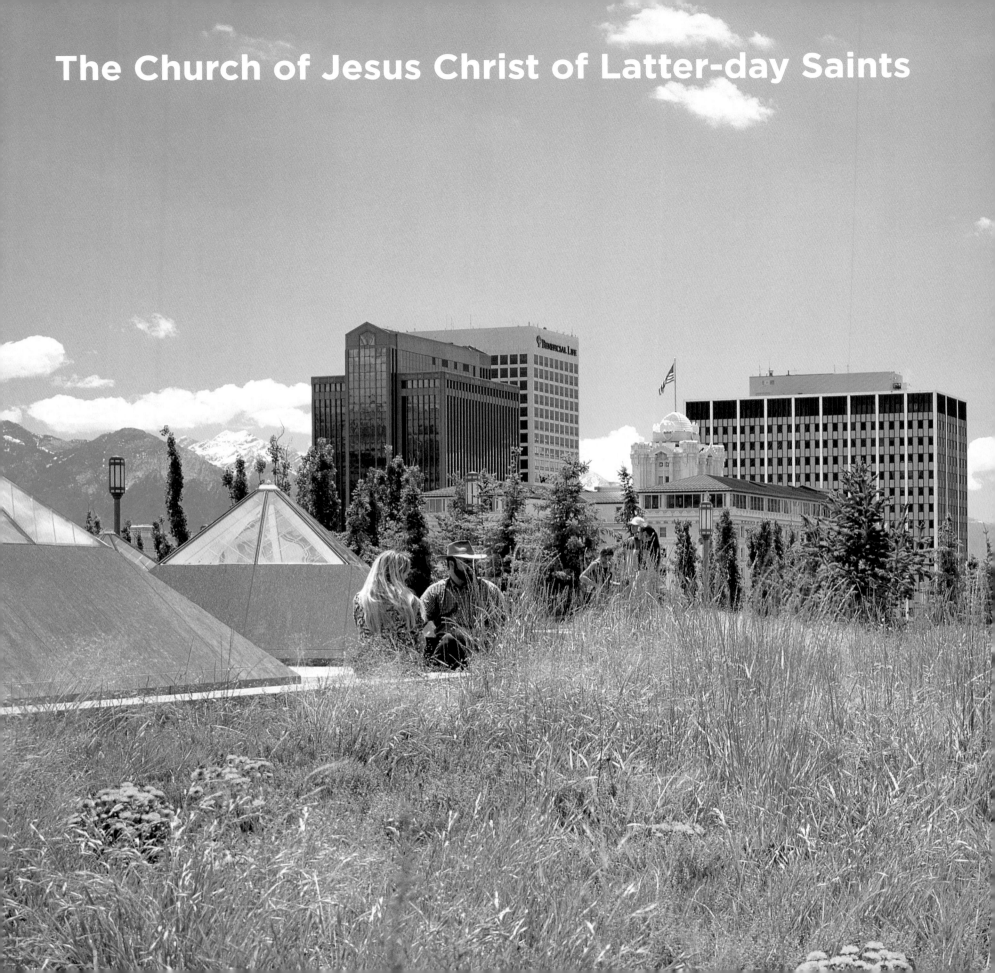

The Church of Jesus Christ of Latter-day Saints

The Church of Jesus Christ of Latter-day Saints Conference Center | **Salt Lake City, Utah** | The principal urban design motive for the Conference Center was to extend the vision of the adjacent Temple Square, while honoring the Temple, the spiritual center of the Mormon Church. The 10-acre site accommodates a 21,000-seat assembly and performance hall, a 900-seat theater, and a parking garage. An easily accessed six-acre roof garden overlooks Temple Square, with its promenade focusing on the Temple itself. The natural landscape of the roof garden evokes an alpine meadow, reminiscent of much of rural Utah.

University of Oregon

University of Oregon | **Athletic Medicine Center** | **Eugene, Oregon** | Occupying 15,000 square feet within the University of Oregon's Len Casanova Athletic Center, the Athletic Medicine Center is a state-of-the-art sports therapy and training facility for more than 400 student-athletes. It features space for treadmills and exercise bikes, hydro-therapy tubs, a nutrition bar, custom-designed massage and taping tables, medical examination suites, an X-ray facility, a student seating area, and meeting rooms. The facility is intended to apply a holistic approach to student-athlete health, with the architecture and materials infused at every turn to showcase the legacy and heritage of the University's athletes.

The University of Oregon's "O" logo, which reinforces the school's brand and rich athletic history, is reflected throughout the center, from the custom-designed steel bar stools to the circular Ingo Mauer light fixtures above the taping tables.

Zimmer Gunsul Frasca

University of Texas at Dallas

University of Texas at Dallas | Natural Science and Engineering Research Building | Dallas, Texas | UT Dallas has invested in expanding the campus to become one of the nation's top research institutions. The centerpiece of the plan provides multidisciplinary research programs, ranging from physics, biology, and chemistry to electrical engineering and neuroscience. The building is sited at the campus' north entry and is the terminus of a major pedestrian mall. Its shape responds to a natural creek that runs through the campus. The communal parts of the program are located at the building ends, including conference rooms on the east and a two-story café and seminar room at the south overlooking a courtyard. Interconnecting stairs are located at the intersection of two building wings. Whether in a laboratory or administrative office area, one can see all the way through the building. A curved glass curtain wall exploits views. The predominant buff-colored pre-cast concrete contextually links the building to the existing campus. Metal panels and colored stainless steel shingles applied to different areas help reduce the building's scale and add interest.

The emphasis on interaction is reflected in the building's interior. Offices are directly adjacent to laboratories, and open stairs are located at the intersection of the two building wings near shared facilities.

Large windows in the laboratories overlook open work stations, allowing those outside to observe experiments in progress. At the back of each laboratory module a service corridor runs the perimeter of the building.

Justice Center,
Portland, Oregon

Chronology

2011   **City Creek Center**
SALT LAKE CITY, UTAH

Oregon State University
Linus Pauling Science Center
CORVALLIS, OREGON

Portland State University
School of Business Administration
PORTLAND, OREGON

Conrad N. Hilton Foundation
New Office Campus
AGOURA HILLS, CALIFORNIA

Children's Memorial Hospital
Ann and Robert H. Lurie Children's Hospital
of Chicago
CHICAGO, ILLINOIS

University of Cincinnati, Social & Behavioral
Sciences Center
CINCINNATI, OHIO

The University of Texas at Arlington,
Engineering Research Building
ARLINGTON, TEXAS

Duke University Medical Center & Health
System, Duke Hospital Expansion
DURHAM, NORTH CAROLINA

Duke University, Nicholas School of the
Environment and Earth Sciences
DURHAM, NORTH CAROLINA

2010   **Soka University of America, New Performing**
Arts Center and Associated Academic
Facilities
ALISO VIEJO, CALIFORNIA

Dana-Farber Cancer Institute, Yawkey Center
for Cancer Care
BOSTON, MASSACHUSETTS

University of Virginia, The UVa Emily Couric
Clinical Cancer Center
CHARLOTTESVILLE, VIRGINIA

Providence Everett Medical Center
EVERETT, WASHINGTON

University of California, Berkeley, Li Ka-Shing
Center for Biomedical and Health Sciences
BERKELEY, CALIFORNIA

Legacy Hospital and Health Center, Emanuel
Children's Hospital
PORTLAND, OREGON

Metro Mid-City / Expo Light Rail
Transit Project
LOS ANGELES, CALIFORNIA

J. Craig Venter Institute
LA JOLLA, CALIFORNIA

2009   **Northwestern University, Richard and**
Barbara Silverman Hall for Molecular
Therapeutics & Diagnostics
EVANSTON, ILLINOIS

Childrens Hospital Los Angeles,
New Patient Tower
LOS ANGELES, CALIFORNIA

Peoria Riverfront Museum and Caterpillar
Visitor Center
PEORIA, ILLINOIS

12 / W Tower
PORTLAND, OREGON

Seattle Children's Hospital and Regional
Medical Center Expansion
SEATTLE, WASHINGTON

North Carolina Cancer Hospital
CHAPEL HILL, NORTH CAROLINA

University of Alaska Anchorage, Integrated
Science Facility
ANCHORAGE, ALASKA

Port of Portland Office Building and Portland
International Airport Parking Garage
PORTLAND, OREGON

Children's Hospital Leukemia Center
BEIJING, CHINA

Clif Bar Headquarters
ALAMEDA, CALIFORNIA

Portland Transit Mall Revitalization
PORTLAND, OREGON

University of Southern California, Broad
Institute for Integrative Biology and
Stem Cell Research
LOS ANGELES, CALIFORNIA

Bellevue Regional Library,
Bellevue, Washington

California Science Center Phase 2, World of Ecology
LOS ANGELES, CALIFORNIA

City of Hope National Medical Center, Advanced Molecular Therapies Center
DUARTE, CALIFORNIA

The University of Hawaii, Cancer Research Center of Hawaii
HONOLULU, HAWAII

Hackensack University Medical Center, Outpatient Cancer Center
HACKENSACK, NEW JERSEY

Iowa State University Biorenewables Complex
AMES, IOWA

2008 **Providence Portland Cancer Center**
PORTLAND, OREGON

The University of Chicago, Knapp Center for Biomedical Discovery
CHICAGO, ILLINOIS

Dickinson College, New Science Facilities
CARLISLE, PENNSYLVANIA

Three Downtown Parks
PORTLAND, OREGON

Science Center, 3711 Market Street
PHILADELPHIA, PENNSYLVANIA

St. Anthony Hospital
GIG HARBOR, WASHINGTON

DC Streetcar, Anacostia Line
WASHINGTON, DC

University of California, Davis, Mondavi Institute for Wine & Food Science
DAVIS, CALIFORNIA

Children's Medical Center Legacy
PLANO, TEXAS

2007 **The Children's Hospital**
DENVER, COLORADO

University of Oregon, Athletic Medicine Center
EUGENE, OREGON

FuWai Hospital of Cardiovascular Disease
BEIJING, CHINA

U.S. Environmental Protection Agency, Region 8 Headquarters
DENVER, COLORADO

University of Texas at Dallas, Natural Science and Engineering Research Building
DALLAS, TEXAS

University of California, Berkeley, Stanley Hall
BERKELEY, CALIFORNIA

BJC HealthCare, Missouri Baptist Medical Center Addition and Renovation
ST. LOUIS, MISSOURI

University of Arizona, Thomas W. Keating Bioresearch Building and Medical Research Building
TUCSON, ARIZONA

Jonathan Rose Companies, Joseph Vance Building
SEATTLE, WASHINGTON

2006 **University of Arizona, Chemical Sciences Building**
TUCSON, ARIZONA

Memorial Sloan-Kettering Cancer Center, The Mortimer B. Zuckerman Research Center (Phase I)
NEW YORK, NEW YORK

The Eliot Tower
PORTLAND, OREGON

Oregon Health & Science University, Biomedical Research Building
PORTLAND, OREGON

Portland State University, Northwest Center for Engineering, Science and Technology
PORTLAND, OREGON

Washington and Lee University, Art and Music Building
LEXINGTON, VIRGINIA

Western Gateway Park
DES MOINES, IOWA

2005 **University of California, San Diego, Rebecca and John Moores UCSD Cancer Center**
SAN DIEGO, CALIFORNIA

Legacy Salmon Creek Hospital
VANCOUVER, WASHINGTON

Washington State University, Plant Biosciences Building
PULLMAN, WASHINGTON

Science Center of Iowa & Blank IMAX® Dome Theater
DES MOINES, IOWA

Carnegie Institution, Maxine F. Singer Building
BALTIMORE, MARYLAND

Pacific Lutheran University, Morken Center for Learning and Technology
TACOMA, WASHINGTON

University of Michigan, Ann and Robert H. Lurie Biomedical Engineering Building Addition
ANN ARBOR, MICHIGAN

2004 **M.D. Anderson Cancer Center, George and Cynthia Mitchell Basic Sciences Research Building**
HOUSTON, TEXAS

University of California, San Diego, Leichtag Family Foundation Biomedical Research Building
SAN DIEGO, CALIFORNIA

San Diego State University, Transit Center
SAN DIEGO, CALIFORNIA

Cornell University, Duffield Hall Nanotechnology Research Facility
ITHACA, NEW YORK

Duke University, Fitzpatrick Center for Interdisciplinary Engineering, Medicine and Applied Sciences
DURHAM, NORTH CAROLINA

National Institutes of Health, Mark O. Hatfield Clinical Research Center
BETHESDA, MARYLAND

Washington Park Station, MAX
Westside Light Rail, Portland, Oregon

University of California, Santa Barbara, Marine Sciences Building
SANTA BARBARA, CALIFORNIA

Fourth & Madison Tower
SEATTLE, WASHINGTON

Iowa State University, Gerdin Business Building
AMES, IOWA

Fred Hutchinson Cancer Research Center (Phases 2-5)
SEATTLE, WASHINGTON

2003 U.S. Consulate Compound
ISTANBUL, TURKEY

Exposition Park Intergenerational Community Center, John C. Argue Swim Stadium
LOS ANGELES, CALIFORNIA

Perkins Coie, LLP
PORTLAND, OREGON

U.S. Food and Drug Administration, FDA at Irvine, Regional Laboratory and District Office
IRVINE, CALIFORNIA

2002 Northwestern University, Center for Nanofabrication and Molecular Self-Assembly
EVANSTON, ILLINOIS

University of California, Santa Barbara, Donald Bren School of Environmental Science and Management and Marine Sciences Building
SANTA BARBARA, CALIFORNIA

University of San Francisco, Mission Bay, Genentech Hall
SAN FRANCISCO, CALIFORNIA

Washington State University, Vancouver Campus
VANCOUVER, WASHINGTON

Ray Quinney & Nebeker, PC
SALT LAKE CITY, UTAH

Portland International Airport
PORTLAND, OREGON

University of California, Riverside, Entomology Building
RIVERSIDE, CALIFORNIA

Everett Station
EVERETT, WASHINGTON

2001 Safeco Insurance Companies, Redmond Campus Expansion
REDMOND, WASHINGTON

Williams College, The Science Center and Schow Science Library
WILLIAMSTOWN, MASSACHUSETTS

Santa Monica Boulevard Master Plan
WEST HOLLYWOOD, CALIFORNIA

2000 Dr. Donald and Beret Mott Children's Center
PUYALLUP, WASHINGTON

The Church of Jesus Christ of Latter-day Saints, Conference Center
SALT LAKE CITY, UTAH

Microsoft Cafeteria
REDMOND, WASHINGTON

1999 The Johns Hopkins University, Bunting-Blaustein Cancer Research Building
BALTIMORE, MARYLAND

1998 MAX Westside Light Rail
PORTLAND, OREGON

Doernbecher Children's Hospital
PORTLAND, OREGON

California Science Center Phase 1
LOS ANGELES, CALIFORNIA

Ronald Reagan Federal Building and U.S. Courthouse
SANTA ANA, CALIFORNIA

1997 William R. Wiley Environmental Sciences Laboratory
RICHLAND, WASHINGTON

1996 University of California, Santa Barbara, Humanities and Social Sciences Building
SANTA BARBARA, CALIFORNIA

Microsoft, Redmond West Campus
REDMOND, WASHINGTON

1995 Peninsula Center Library
PALOS VERDES, CALIFORNIA

Pacific Lutheran University, Mary Baker Russell Music Center
TACOMA, WASHINGTON

1994 University of California, San Diego, Engineering Building Unit II
SAN DIEGO, CALIFORNIA

1993 Bellevue Regional Library
BELLEVUE, WASHINGTON

Fred Hutchinson Cancer Research Center (Phase 1)
SEATTLE, WASHINGTON

1992 Oregon Museum of Science and Industry
PORTLAND, OREGON

University of California, Irvine Engineering Unit 2
IRVINE, CALIFORNIA

1991 Safeco Center
SEATTLE, WASHINGTON

1990 Oregon Convention Center
PORTLAND, OREGON

1989 Reed College, Hauser Library
PORTLAND, OREGON

1988 The Link
KANSAS CITY, MISSOURI

1987 Oregon Health & Science University, Vollum Institute
PORTLAND, OREGON

Bonneville Power Administration
PORTLAND, OREGON

1986 MAX Banfield Light Rail
PORTLAND, OREGON

1984 KOIN Center
PORTLAND, OREGON

1983 Justice Center
PORTLAND, OREGON

Credits

Carnegie Institution
Maxine F. Singer Building
BALTIMORE, MARYLAND
Client: **Carnegie Institution**
Mechanical/Electrical/Plumbing Engineer: **RMF Engineering, Inc.**
Structural Engineer: **Robert Silman Associates, P.C.**
Landscape Architect: **EDAW, Inc.**
Laboratory Planner: **SST Planners**
Contractor: **Clark Construction Group, LLC**
Photographers: **Alan Karchmer/ESTO; Maxwell MacKenzie**

Cornell University
Duffield Hall Nanotechnology Research Facility
ITHACA, NEW YORK
Client: **Cornell University**
Mechanical/Electrical/Plumbing Engineer: **Bard, Rao + Athanas Consulting Engineers, LLC**
Structural Engineer: **LeMessurier Consultants**
Landscape Architect: **EDAW, Inc.**
Laboratory Planner: **Earl Walls Associates**
Lighting Designer: **Francis Krahe & Associates, Inc.**
Contractors: **McCarthy Building Companies, Inc.;Welliver McGuire**
Photographers: **Robert Canfield Photography; Larry Falke/Falke Photography; Jon Reis**

Dr. Donald and Beret Mott Children's Center
PUYALLUP, WASHINGTON
Client: **Good Samaritan Hospital**
Mechanical Design Engineer of Record: **Path Engineers**
Design/Build Mechanical Contractor: **W. A. Botting Company**
Electrical Design Engineer of Record: **Tres West Engineers, Inc.**
Design/Build Electrical Contractor: **McMullen Electric, Inc.**
Structural Engineer: **PCS Structural Solutions**
Landscape Architect: **Blue Sky Landscaping Services, Inc.**
Artists: **Lynn Goodpasture, Charles Fitzgerald, Michelle Van Slyke**
Pool Consultants: **Pyramid Pools; and TMI Salt Pure**
Contractor: **Absher Construction Company**
Photographer: **Eckert & Eckert**

Duke University
Fitzpatrick Center for Interdisciplinary Engineering, Medicine and Applied Sciences
DURHAM, NORTH CAROLINA
Client: **Duke University**
Mechanical/Electrical/Plumbing Engineer: **Bard, Rao + Athanas Consulting Engineers, LLC**
Structural Engineer: **Cagley & Associates**
Landscape Architect: **EDAW, Inc.**
Laboratory Planners: **Jacobs Consultancy/GPR Planners Collaborative, Inc.**
Clean Room Consultant: **Abbie Gregg, Inc.**
Construction Manager: **Skanska USA Building, Inc.**
Photographers: **Alan Karchmer/ESTO; Timothy Hurlsey/The Arkansas Office; Chuck Choi**

Exposition Park Intergenerational Community Center
John C. Argue Swim Stadium
LOS ANGELES, CALIFORNIA
Client: **Exposition Park Intergenerational Community Center**
Owner's Representative: **Beck Madson Associates, Inc.**
Structural/Mechanical/Electrical/Plumbing Engineer: **ARUP**
Landscape Architect: **Katherine Spitz and Associates**
Historical Consultant: **Offenhauser/Mekeel Architects**
Pool Consultant: **Rowley International, Inc.**
Artists: **Elizabeth Garrison; Victor Henderson**
Contractor: **CW Driver**
Photographer: **Timothy Hursley/The Arkansas Office**

California Science Center,
Los Angeles, California

Fourth & Madison Tower

SEATTLE, WASHINGTON

Client: **Hines Interests Limited Partnership**

Design Architect: **Zimmer Gunsul Frasca Architects LLP**

Architect of Record: **Kendall/Heaton Associates, Inc.**

Mechanical/Electrical Engineer: **Flack + Kurtz, Inc.**

Structural Engineer: **Magnusson Klemencic & Associates**

Artist: **James Carpenter Design Associates, Inc.**

Graphics/Wayfinding: **Hornall Anderson Design Works, Inc.**

Contractor: **PCL Construction Services, Inc.**

Photographers: **Eckert & Eckert; AZ Photo; Lara Swimmer**

Fred Hutchinson Cancer Research Center

SEATTLE, WASHINGTON

Client: **Fred Hutchinson Cancer Research Center**

Mechanical/Electrical/Plumbing Engineer: **Affiliated Engineers, Inc.**

Structural Engineer: **KPFF Consulting Engineers, Inc.**

Landscape Architects: **Jones & Jones; Brumbaugh & Associates; Murase Associates**

Graphics/Wayfinding: **Hornall Anderson Design Works, Inc.**

Laboratory Planner: **AHSC McLellan Copenhagen, LLC**

Contractors: **Koll Company; Turner Construction Company**

Photographer: **Eckert & Eckert; Doug Scott Photography**

Iowa State University
Gerdin Business Building

AMES, IOWA

Client: **Iowa State University**

Mechanical/Electrical/Plumbing Engineer: **Farris Engineering**

Structural Engineer: **KPFF Consulting Engineers, Inc.**

Contractor: **Miron Construction Company**

Photographers: **Farshid Assassi; Lark, Inc.; Eckert & Eckert**

Legacy Salmon Creek Hospital

VANCOUVER, WASHINGTON

Client: **Legacy Health System**

Mechanical/Electrical/Plumbing Engineer: **Affiliated Engineers, Inc.**

Structural Engineer: **KPFF Consulting Engineers, Inc.**

Landscape Architect: **Walker Macy**

Medical Planner: **James Brinkley**

Artists: **Ann Gardner; Lutz Haufschild; Lee Kelly; Michihiro Kosuge; Judith Poxson Fawkes**

Fountain Designer: **Waterscape Solutions**

Graphics/Wayfinding: **Anderson Krygier, Inc.**

Lighting Designer: **Francis Krahe & Associates, Inc.**

Contractor: **Skanska USA Building, Inc.**

Photographer: **Eckert & Eckert; Robert Canfield Photography**

Memorial Sloan-Kettering Cancer Center
The Mortimer B. Zuckerman Research Center

NEW YORK, NEW YORK

Client: **Memorial Sloan-Kettering Cancer Center**

Owner's Representative: **Granary Associates**

Associate Architect: **Skidmore Owings & Merrill LLP**

Mechanical/Electrical/Plumbing Engineers: **Affiliated Engineers, Inc.; Cosentini Associates**

Structural Engineer: **Skidmore Owings & Merrill LLP**

Laboratory Planner: **Jacobs Consultancy / GPR Planners Collaborative, Inc.**

Lighting Designer: **Cline Bettridge Bernstein Lighting Design, Inc.**

Artists: **Alyson Shotz; Jim Isermann**

Construction Manager: **Turner Construction Company**

Photographer: **David Sundberg/ESTO**

Microsoft Cafeteria

REDMOND, WASHINGTON

Client: **Microsoft Corporation**

Mechanical/Electrical/Plumbing Engineer: **Coffman Engineers**

Structural Engineer: **KPFF Consulting Engineers**

Landscape Architect: **Brumbaugh & Associates**

Data/Communications: **COMgroup, Inc.**

Artist: **Sol LeWitt**

Contractor: **Sellen Construction Company**

Photographer: **Richard Strode/Strode Photographic**

National Institutes of Health
Mark O. Hatfield Clinical Research Center

BETHESDA, MARYLAND

Client: **National Institutes of Health**

Development Manager: **Boston Properties**

Mechanical/Electrical/Plumbing Engineer: **Affiliated Engineers, Inc.**

Structural Engineer: **Cagley & Associates**

Landscape Architect: **EDAW, Inc.**

Medical Planning: **NBBJ**

Radiation Oncology: **Tobey + Davis**

Laboratory Planners: **Earl Walls Associates; AHSC McLellan Copenhagen, LLC**

Graphics/Wayfinding: **The Douglas Group**

Lighting Designer: **Domingo Gonzalez Design**

Materials Handling/Management: **KDA Group**

Medical Equipment / Medical Telecommunications: **Gene Burton & Associates**

Artist: **Larry Kirkland Studio**

Construction Manager: **Centex Construction Company**

Photographer: **Alan Karchmer/ESTO**

Oregon Health & Science University
Biomedical Research Building
PORTLAND, OREGON

Client: **Oregon Health & Science University**
Owner's Representative: **Ethos Development, Inc.**
Mechanical/Electrical/Plumbing Engineer: **Affiliated Engineers, Inc.**
Structural Engineer: **KPFF Consulting Engineers, Inc.**
Laboratory Planner: **Jacobs Consultancy/GPR Planners Collaborative, Inc.**
Lighting Designer: **Francis Krahe & Associates, Inc.**
MRIs: **NMR Magnex Scientific, Inc.**
Contractor: **Hoffman Construction Company**
Photographer: **Eckert & Eckert**

Pacific Lutheran University
Morken Center for Learning and Technology
TACOMA, WASHINGTON

Client: **Pacific Lutheran University**
Owner's Representative: **Lorig Associates, LLC**
Mechanical/Electrical/Plumbing Engineer: **PAE Consulting Engineers, Inc.**
Structural Engineer: **Coughlin Porter Lundeen**
LEED Commissioning: **Engineering Economics, Inc.**
Graphics/Wayfinding: **Mayer/Reed**
Contractor: **Sellen Construction Company**
Photographers: **Eckert & Eckert; John Edwards**

Perkins Coie, LLP
PORTLAND, OREGON

Client: **Perkins Coie, LLP**
Mechanical/Electrical/Plumbing Engineer: **Glumac International**
Structural Engineer: **KPFF Consulting Engineers, Inc.**
Lighting Designer: **Francis Krahe & Associates, Inc.**
Contractor: **Skanska USA Building, Inc.**
Photographer: **Nick Merrick © Hedrich Blessing**

Portland International Airport
Terminal Expansion
PORTLAND, OREGON

Client: **Port of Portland**
Associate Architect (Terminal Access Program): **Fletcher Farr Ayotte, PC**
Mechanical/Electrical: **PAE Consulting Engineers, Inc.**
Structural Engineer: **KPFF Consulting Engineers, Inc.**
Landscape Architect: **Mayer/Reed**
Artist: **Larry Kirkland Studios**
Graphics/Wayfinding: **Debra Nichols Design; Design Partnership; Mayer/Reed**
Lighting Designer: **Fisher Marantz Stone**
Contractors: **Skanska USA Building, Inc.; Hoffman Construction Company**
Photographers: **Eckert & Eckert; Timothy Hursley/The Arkansas Office**

Portland State University
Northwest Center for Engineering, Science and Technology
PORTLAND, OREGON

Client: **Portland State University**
Owner's Representative: **Gerdin/Edlen Development Company**
Mechanical/Electrical/Plumbing Engineer: **PAE Consulting Engineers, Inc.**
Structural Engineer: **KPFF Consulting Engineers, Inc.**
Landscape Architect: **Walker Macy**
Programming: **University Planning Associates**
Laboratory Planner: **Earl Walls Associates**
Lighting Designer: **Luma Lighting Design**
Artist: **Ed Carpenter Studios**
Graphics/Wayfinding: **Anderson Krygier, Inc.**
Contractor: **Lease Crutcher Lewis**
Photographer: **Eckert & Eckert**

Ray Quinney & Nebeker, PC
SALT LAKE CITY, UTAH

Client: **Ray Quinney & Nebeker, PC**
Architectural Woodworking: **Fetzers**
Masonry Wall: **H & P Tile**
Graphics/Wayfinding: **Wadsworth**
Contractor: **Greenwood Construction**
Photographer: **Richard Barnes**

Ronald Reagan Federal Building and U.S. Courthouse

SANTA ANA, CALIFORNIA

Client: **U.S. General Services Administration**

Design Architect: **Zimmer Gunsul Frasca Architects LLP**

Architect of Record: **Gruen Associates**

Mechanical Engineer: **Tsuchiyama & Kaino Consulting Mechanical Engineers**

Electrical Engineer: **Frederick Brown & Associates**

Structural Engineer: **Martin & Huang International, Inc.**

Lighting Designer: **Francis Krahe & Associates, Inc.**

Artists: **John Valdez; Raymond Kaskey**

Graphics/Wayfinding: **Follis Design**

Contractor: **Ray Wilson Company**

Photographer: **Timothy Hursley/The Arkansas Office**

**Safeco Insurance Companies
Redmond Campus Expansion**

REDMOND, WASHINGTON

Client: **Safeco Insurance Companies**

Mechanical Engineer: **McKinstry Company**

Electrical Engineer: **Sparling**

Structural Engineer: **KPFF Consulting Engineers, Inc.**

Landscape Architect: **Brumbaugh & Associates**

Artist: **James Carpenter Design Associates, Inc.**

Graphics/Wayfinding: **Mayer/Reed**

Contractor: **Skanska USA Building, Inc.**

Photographers: **Nick Merrick © Hedrich Blessing; Steve Keating; Doug Scott**

**San Diego State University
Transit Center**

SAN DIEGO, CALIFORNIA

Client: **Metropolitan Transit Development Board
(now Metropolitan Transit System)**

Prime Contractor: **BRW Group/URS Corporation**

Electrical Engineer: **W.J. Yang and Associates**

Utilities Engineer: **Lintvedt, McColl & Associates; Randall Lamb Associates**

Structural Engineer: **INCA Engineers**

Landscape Architect: **Estrada Land Planning**

Artist: **Anne Mudge**

Tunnel Engineer: **Hatch Mott MacDonald**

Contractor: **Clark Construction Group, LLC**

Photographer: **Larry Falke/Falke Photography**

Science Center of Iowa & Blank IMAX® DomeTheater

DES MOINES, IOWA

Client: **Science Center of Iowa**

Mechanical/Electrical/Plumbing/Structural Engineer: **Brooks Borg Skiles Architecture Engineering LLP**

Mechanical Subcontractor to BBS: **The Waldinger Corporation**

Electrical Subcontractor to BBS: **Baker Electric, Inc.**

Museum Programmer/Planner: **White Oak Associates, Inc.**

Exhibit Design: **Design + Communications**

Theater Consultant: **IMAX Corporation**

Acoustics: **Purcell + Noppe + Associates, Inc.**

Fountain Consultant: **The Fountain People**

Contractor: **Neumann Brothers, Inc.**

Photographers: **Timothy Hursley/The Arkansas Office; Eckert & Eckert**

The Children's Hospital

DENVER, COLORADO

Client: **The Children's Hospital**

Program Managers: **Balfour Concord**

Design Architect: **Zimmer Gunsul Frasca Architects LLP**

Architect of Record: **H+L Architecture**

Structural/Civil Engineer: **S.A. Miro, Inc.**

Landscape Architect: **EDAW**

Design Mechanical/Electrical/Plumbing Engineer: **Bard, Rao + Athanas Consulting Engineers, LLC**

Associate Mechanical/Electrical/Plumbing Engineer: **Cator, Ruma & Associates**

Medical Equipment Planner: **CPI Group, LLC**

Food Service: **Systems Design International**

Vertical Transportation: **Lerch, Bates & Associates**

Acoustics and Vibration: **Colin Gordon & Associates**

Security Design: **Kroll Security Services Group**

Information Technology: **Sparling and Rimrock Group, Inc.**

Lighting Designer: **Francis Krahe & Associates, Inc.**

Art Consultant: **Eloise Damrosch**

Commissioned Artists: **Duke Beardsley, Carolyn Braaksma, John Buck, Jim Buddish, John Fielder, Larry Kirkland, Patty Maly, Jesus Moroles, Karen Story, Mary Williams**

Art Glass Production: **Skyline Design**

Graphics/Wayfinding: **Arthouse Design**

Contractor: **Phipps/McCarthy**

Photographer: **Eckert & Eckert; Basil Childers**

The Church of Jesus Christ of Latter-day Saints
Conference Center
SALT LAKE CITY, UTAH
Client: **The Church of Jesus Christ of Latter-day Saints**
Associate Architect: **Gillies Stransky Brems Smith Architects**
Mechanical/Electrical/Plumbing Engineer: **CHP & Associates, Consulting Engineers, Inc.**
Structural Engineer: **KPFF Consulting Engineers, Inc.**
Landscape Architect: **Olin Partnership**
Fountain: **CMS Collaborative**
Acoustics: **Jaffe Holden Acoustics, Inc.**
Audio/Visual: **National TeleConsultants**
Theater Consultant: **Auerbach + Associates**
Lighting Designer: **Auerbach + Glasow**
Contractor: **Legacy Constructors**
Photographers: **Timothy Hursley/The Arkansas Office; Eckert & Eckert**

The Eliot Tower
PORTLAND, OREGON
Client: **Carroll Investments, LLC**
Design Architect: **Zimmer Gunsul Frasca Architects LLP**
Architect of Record: **Ankrom Moisan Associated Architects**
Interior Design: **Soderberg Laman Designers (Residential Units); Ankrom Moisan Associated Architects (Residential Units/Public Spaces); Zimmer Gunsul Frasca Architects LLP (Lobby)**
Mechanical/Electrical/Plumbing Engineer: **Glumac International**
Structural Engineer: **KPFF Consulting Engineers, Inc.**
Contractor: **Howard S. Wright Construction Company**
Photographers: **Rick Keating; Eckert & Eckert**

U.S. Consulate Compound
ISTANBUL, TURKEY
Client: **U.S. Department of State**
Mechanical/Electrical/Plumbing Engineer: **Syska Hennessy Group, Inc.**
Structural/Civil Engineer: **KPFF Consulting Engineers, Inc.**
Landscape Architect: **EDAW, Inc.**
Artist: **Maya Lin**
Graphics/Wayfinding: **Mayer/Reed**
Lighting Designer: **Fisher Marantz Stone**
Security Consultant: **Jaycor**
Contractor: **Caddell Construction Co., Inc.**
Photographer: **Christian Richters**

U.S. Environmental Protection Agency
Region 8 Headquarters
DENVER, COLORADO
Client: **Opus Northwest**
Tenant: **U.S. Environmental Protection Agency**
Tenant's Representative: **U.S. General Services Administration**
Design Architect: **Zimmer Gunsul Frasca Architects LLP**
Architect of Record: **Opus A&E, Inc.**
Consulting Architect: **Shears Adkins Architects, LLC**
Landscape Architect: **Zimmer Gunsul Frasca Architects LLP**
Structural Engineer: **KPFF Consulting Engineers, Inc.**
Civil Engineer: **Martin/Martin Consulting Engineers**
Mechanical/Electrical/Plumbing Engineer of Record: **Syska Hennessy Group, Inc.**
Mechanical Engineer: **Doyle Engineering, Inc.**
Electrical Engineer: **BCER Engineering, Inc.**
Lighting Designer: **Keylight + Shadow**
Sails Fabrication: **North Winds Canvas**
Sails Installation: **Rhino Rigging**
Photographer: **Robert Canfield Photography**

U.S. Food and Drug Administration
FDA at Irvine, Regional Laboratory and District Office
IRVINE, CALIFORNIA
Client: **U.S. Food and Drug Administration**
Design: **Joint venture of Zimmer Gunsul Frasca Architects LLP and Henningson Durham & Richardson**
Architects: **Zimmer Gunsul Frasca Architects LLP**
Building Engineering: **Henningson, Durham & Richardson**
Laboratory Planner: **Earl Walls Associates**
Contractor: **Hensel Phelps Construction Company**
Construction Manager: **Gilbane Building Company**
Photographers: **Adrian Velicescu/Standard; Nick Merrick © Hedrich Blessing; Eckert & Eckert**

University of Arizona
Chemical Sciences Building
TUCSON, ARIZONA
Client: **University of Arizona**
Mechanical/Electrical/Plumbing Engineer: **Affiliated Engineers, Inc.**
Structural Engineers: **Holben, Martin & White Consulting Structural Engineers, Inc.; John A. Martin & Associates, Inc.**
Landscape Architect: **Katherine Spitz and Associates**
Laboratory Planner: **Earl Walls Associates**
Lighting Designer: **Francis Krahe & Associates, Inc.**
Contractor: **Hensel Phelps Construction Company**
Photographer: **Robert Canfield Photography**

University of Arizona
Thomas W. Keating Bioresearch Building and Medical Research Building
TUCSON, ARIZONA
Client: **University of Arizona**
Mechanical/Electrical/Plumbing Engineer: **Affiliated Engineers, Inc.**
Structural Engineers: **Holben, Martin & White Consulting Structural Engineers, Inc./John A. Martin & Associates, Inc. (building); KPFF Consulting Engineers, Inc. (ramada)**
Landscape Architect: **Wheat Scharf Associates**
Laboratory Planner: **Earl Walls Associates**
Lighting Designer: **Francis Krahe & Associates, Inc.**
Contractors: **Gilbane (Keating Bioresearch); Hensel Phelps Construction Company (Medical Research)**
Photographers: **Robert Canfield Photography; Adrian Velicescu/Standard**

University of California, Berkeley
Stanley Hall
BERKELEY, CALIFORNIA
Client: **University of California, Berkeley**
Mechanical/Electrical/Plumbing Engineer: **Bard, Rao + Athanas Consulting Engineers, LLC**
Structural Engineer: **Rutherford & Chekene**
Landscape Architect: **Murase Associates**
Laboratory Planner: **Research Facilities Design**
Contractor: **McCarthy Building Companies, Inc.**
Photographer: **Robert Canfield Photography**

University of California, Riverside
Entomology Building
RIVERSIDE, CALIFORNIA
Client: **University of California, Riverside**
Mechanical/Electrical/Plumbing Engineer: **Affiliated Engineers, Inc.**
Structural/Civil Engineer: **KPFF Consulting Engineers, Inc.**
Landscape Architect: **Katherine Spitz and Associates**
Laboratory Planner: **AHSC McLellan Copenhagen, LLC**
Contractor: **Skidmore Contracting Company**
Photographer: **Timothy Hursley/The Arkansas Office**

University of California, San Diego
Leichtag Family Foundation Biomedical Research Building
SAN DIEGO, CALIFORNIA
Client: **University of California, San Diego**
Mechanical/Electrical/Plumbing Engineer: **Fundament and Associates, Inc.**
Structural Engineer: **KPFF Consulting Engineers, Inc.**
Landscape Architect: **Katherine Spitz and Associates**
Artist: **Ed Carpenter Studios**
Laboratory Planner: **Earl Walls Associates**
Lighting Designer: **Pacific Lightworks, LLC**
Contractor: **McCarthy Building Companies, Inc.**
Photographer: **Robert Canfield Photography**

University of California, San Diego
Rebecca and John Moores UCSD Cancer Center
SAN DIEGO, CALIFORNIA
Client: **University of California, San Diego**
Mechanical/Electrical/Plumbing Engineer: **Affiliated Engineers, Inc.**
Structural Engineer: **KPFF Consulting Engineers, Inc.**
Landscape Architect: **Katherine Spitz and Associates**
Laboratory Planner: **Earl Walls Associates**
Lighting Designer: **Francis Krahe & Associates, Inc.**
Contractor: **McCarthy Building Companies, Inc.**
Photographers: **Nick Merrick © Hedrich Blessing; Adrian Velicescu/Standard; Robert Canfield Photography**

University of California, Santa Barbara
Donald Bren School of Environmental Science and Management and Marine Sciences Building
SANTA BARBARA, CALIFORNIA
Client: **University of California, Santa Barbara**
Mechanical/Electrical/Plumbing Engineer: **Flack + Kurtz, Inc.**
Structural Engineer: **KPFF Consulting Engineers, Inc.**
Landscape Architect: **Wallace Roberts & Todd, LLC**
Laboratory Planner: **Earl Walls Associates**
Seawater Tanks: **PC Aquatics (now PBS&J, Inc.)**
Contractors: **Soltek Pacific (Bren School); Pinner Construction Company, Inc. (Marine Sciences)**
Photographers: **Timothy Hursley/The Arkansas Office; Adrian Velicescu/Standard; Robert Canfield Photography**

Oregon Convention Center,
Portland, Oregon

Zimmer Gunsul Frasca

University of Michigan
Ann and Robert H. Lurie Biomedical Engineering Building Addition
ANN ARBOR, MICHIGAN
Client: **University of Michigan**
Associate Architect: **Hobbs & Black**
Mechanical/Electrical/Plumbing Engineer: **Bard, Rao + Athanas Consulting Engineers, LLC**
Laboratory Electrical Engineer: **Michael Wall**
Structural Engineer: **KPFF Consulting Engineers, Inc.**
Laboratory Planner: **Research Facilities Design**
Lighting Designer: **Francis Krahe & Associates, Inc.**
Contractor: **Skanska USA Building, Inc.**
Photographers: **Lark, Inc.; Balthazar Korab**

University of Oregon
Athletic Medicine Center
EUGENE, OREGON
Client: **University of Oregon**
Structural Engineer: **KPFF Consulting Engineers, Inc.**
Landscape Architect: **Zimmer Gunsul Frasca Architects LLP**
Mechanical/Electrical/Plumbing Conceptual Design: **Balzhiser & Hubbard Engineers**
Mechanical/Electrical/Plumbing Design-Build: **L.R. Brabham, Inc.**
Lighting Designer: **Glumac**
Environmental Graphics: **Zimmer Gunsul Frasca Architects LLP**
Art Glass Production: **Juno Architectural Glass**
Contractor: **Hoffman Construction Company**
Photographer: **Basil Childers**

University of Texas at Dallas
Natural Science and Engineering Research Building
DALLAS, TEXAS
Client: **University of Texas at Dallas**
Design Architect: **Zimmer Gunsul Frasca Architects LLP**
Architect of Record: **PageSoutherlandPage LLP**
Mechanical/Electrical/Plumbing Engineer: **PageSoutherlandPage LLP**
Structural/Civil Engineer: **Datum Engineers, Inc.**
Landscape Architect: **J. Camille La Foy, ASLA**
Laboratory Planner: **Jacobs Consultancy/GPR Planners Collaborative, Inc.**
Contractor: **Centex Construction Company**
Photographer: **Robert Canfield Photography**

Washington State University
Vancouver Campus
VANCOUVER, WASHINGTON
Client: **Washington State University**
Mechanical/Electrical/Plumbing Engineer: **PAE Consulting Engineers, Inc.**
Structural Engineer: **Kramer Gehlen Associates, Inc.**
Landscape Architects: **Mayer/Reed (Phase I); Zimmer Gunsul Frasca Architects LLP (subsequent phases)**
Audio Visual: **Delta A/V Systems, Inc.**
Graphics/Wayfinding: **Mayer/Reed**
Laboratory Planner: **Earl Walls Associates**
Contractor: **Skanska USA Building, Inc.**
Photographer: **Eckert & Eckert**

Williams College
The Science Center and Schow Science Library
WILLIAMSTOWN, MASSACHUSETTS
Client: **Williams College**
Associate Architect: **Einhorn Yaffee Prescott**
Mechanical/Electrical/Plumbing Engineer: **Einhorn Yaffee Prescott**
Structural Engineer: **Ryan-Biggs Associates, PC**
Landscape Architect: **Carol R. Johnson Associates, Inc.**
Laboratory Planner: **Earl Walls Associates**
Contractor: **Gilbane Building Company**
Photographer: **Timothy Hursley/The Arkansas Office**

Zimmer Gunsul Frasca Architects
Los Angeles Office
LOS ANGELES, CALIFORNIA
Lighting Designer: **Francis Krahe & Associates, Inc.**
Contractor: **Warner Constructors, Inc.**
Photographers: **Nick Merrick © Hedrich Blessing; Robert Canfield Photography; Toshi Yoshimi**

First Edition

Published in the United States of America in 2008 by Balcony Press

Zimmer Gunsul Frasca: Future Tense © 2008 Zimmer Gunsul Frasca Architects LLP

For information address Balcony Media, Inc.
512 E. Wilson Avenue, Suite 213, Glendale, California 91206

Design by Pure+Applied and Leslie Baker Graphic Design
Printing and production by Navigator Cross-media
Printed in South Korea. Recycling is mandatory and South Korea has an aggressive reforestation program.

Library of Congress Control Number: 2008932665
ISBN: 978-1-890449-50-6

Acknowledgments

THE WORKS IN THIS MONOGRAPH date back almost a decade. Whereas the design and execution of previous projects were directed by a relatively small number of us, now a breadth of talented individuals, pervading every corner of the staff, are full partners in the work we do. To name certain individuals would risk overlooking others, and therefore it is appropriate to credit the entire partnership and staff in our five offices and recognize their considerable contribution to the work within these covers. In addition, the consultants with whom we work in the engineering disciplines and allied design professions (artists, landscape architects, laboratory consultants, etc.) have contributed the crucial dimension that adds to the breadth of our work in important ways.

SPECIFIC TO THIS MONOGRAPH, the marketing directors and staff in each of the offices, led by Nancy Fishman, have added their considerable talent and done the hard work of generating and coordinating for publication all that you see here. They can all share in the pride that we feel. Our publishers at Balcony Press, along with graphic designers, Leslie Baker, Urshula Barbour and Paul Carlos have led us through this process with patience and fortitude.

LAST BUT NOT LEAST, we want to express our heartfelt thanks to our clients. They have entrusted us with not only large amounts of their financial resources, but, more importantly, with the culture of their institutions, be they public or private. So for us, this is a telephoto look in the rearview mirror of what we have done in a defined period of time, and blends in our understanding of not only where we have been but where we might be going. We hope you enjoy this collection of work and learn a little bit more of what we are about.

Robert Frasca